What Your Colleagues Are Saying . . .

"Fisher and Frey set the record straight about text-dependent questions. They demonstrate that text-dependent questions can address not only literal understanding but also understandings about what the text doesn't say, how the text works, what the text means to and for the reader, how the text might be read in a specific discipline, and more. With specific prompts and concrete examples, Fisher and Frey show us how to use questioning as a central tool to address the Common Core State Standards."

NELL K. DUKE, EdD
University of Michigan

"Fisher and Frey have a knack for making complex topics accessible. They write in a jargon-free style that teachers appreciate, and their use of examples and analogies helps bring ideas to life. These are qualities their readers have come to expect, and this book does not disappoint. . . . Teachers will find here an abundance of fresh, practical ideas that are easy to implement. This book deserves a 'close read,' and I heartily recommend it."

MICHAEL MCKENNA
University of Virginia

"Doug Fisher and Nancy Frey are experts at linking research to educational practice. Their latest book, *Text-Dependent Questions*, provides teachers with the information they need to scaffold their students' deep comprehension through four levels of questioning. I am excited to share this book with teachers and colleagues!"

LINDA DORN, PhD
University of Arkansas at Little Rock

"*Text-Dependent Questions* solidifies Fisher and Frey's well-earned reputation as literacy experts who offer sane and nuanced interpretations of the Common Core State Standards. They remind us that close reading at its best is a social process, one involving teacher-learner interaction as well as student-to-student talk. While the recommended texts and sample questions are useful, the extended classroom examples are the true heart of the book, demonstrating how skilled practitioners flexibly devise and deploy high-quality questions to serve varied instructional purposes."

KELLY CHANDLER-OLCOTT
Syracuse University

"Fisher and Frey deliver another indispensable resource for teachers of adolescents across the curriculum as they strive to meet today's more rigorous standards. Mentoring students to grow from dependence on questions provided by others to developing the capacity to 'interrogate a text' themselves is fundamental to proficient reading of complex disciplinary texts. *Text-Dependent Questions* provides teachers with a carefully reasoned pathway for questioning a text as a requisite for close reading."

DOUG BUEHL

Author of *Classroom Strategies for Interactive Learning*

"Everything about this book is genuine. From the authors' candid appraisal of the myths surrounding close reading to their forthright recommendations for teaching, it is refreshing. Fisher and Frey have been there, lived the pedagogy, and generated much of the scholarship that makes *Text-Dependent Questions* both compelling and unpretentious. Readers who have heard this dynamic pair speak at conferences and other professional gatherings are in for a treat; Fisher and frey are indisputably on the frontline when it comes to engaging others in close reading."

DONNA E. ALVERMANN

The Omer Clyde & Elizabeth Parr Aderhold Professor in Education
Distinguished Research Professor of Language and Literacy Education

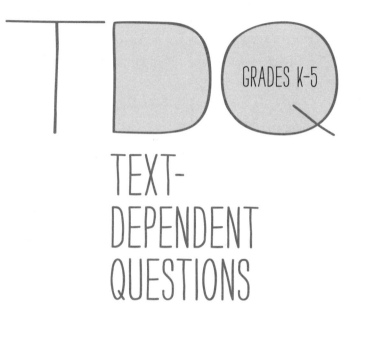

GRADES K-5

TEXT-DEPENDENT QUESTIONS

TDQ

GRADES K-5

TEXT-DEPENDENT QUESTIONS

PATHWAYS TO CLOSE AND CRITICAL READING

DOUGLAS FISHER & NANCY FREY

WITH HEATHER ANDERSON & MARISOL THAYRE

Professional Learning Guide and PowerPoint slides by Laura Hancock available at www.corwin.com/textdependentquestions

CORWIN
LITERACY

FOR INFORMATION:

Corwin

A SAGE Company

2455 Teller Road

Thousand Oaks, California 91320

(800) 233-9936

www.corwin.com

SAGE Publications Ltd.

1 Oliver's Yard

55 City Road

London EC1Y 1SP

United Kingdom

SAGE Publications India Pvt. Ltd.

B 1/I 1 Mohan Cooperative Industrial Area

Mathura Road, New Delhi 110 044

India

SAGE Publications Asia-Pacific Pte. Ltd.

3 Church Street

#10-04 Samsung Hub

Singapore 049483

Photographs by John A. Graham.

Printed in the United States of America.

A catalog record of this book is available from the Library of Congress.

ISBN: 978-1-4833-3131-7

Publisher: Lisa Luedeke

Editorial Development Manager: Julie Nemer

Editorial Assistants: Francesca Dutra Africano and Emeli Warren

Production Editor: Melanie Birdsall

Copy Editor: Cate Huisman

Typesetter: C&M Digitals (P) Ltd.

Proofreader: Victoria Reed-Castro

Indexer: Sheila Bodell

Cover Designer: Gail Buschman

Marketing Manager: Maura Sullivan

This book is printed on acid-free paper.

15 16 17 18 10 9 8 7 6 5 4 3 2

CONTENTS

Chapter 4: What Does the Text *Mean*?   92

Chapter 5: What Does the Text *Inspire You to Do*?   129

- Appendix III: Grades 4–5

NOTE FROM
THE PUBLISHER

The authors have provided links to video and web content throughout the book that is available to you through QR codes. To read a QR code, you must have a smartphone or tablet with a camera. We recommend that you download a QR code reader app that is made specifically for your phone or tablet brand.

QR codes may provide access to videos and/or websites that are not maintained, sponsored, endorsed, or controlled by Corwin. Your use of these third-party websites will be subject to the terms and conditions posted on such websites. Corwin takes no responsibility and assumes no liability for your use of any third-party website. Corwin does not approve, sponsor, endorse, verify, or certify information available at any third-party video or website.

Visit the companion website at
www.corwin.com/textdependentquestions
for the Professional Learning Guide and PowerPoint
slides by Laura Hancock and access to the video clips
and other resources.

ACKNOWLEDGMENTS

Corwin gratefully acknowledges the contributions of the following reviewers:

Nancy Akhavan
Assistant Professor
Department of Educational Research and Administration
California State University, Fresno
Fresno, CA

Jennifer Wheat Townsend
Literacy Specialist
MSD Pike Township
Indianapolis, IN

CREATING *EFFECTIVE* CLOSE READING LESSONS

The students in Matt Taylor's fourth grade class were reading Ernest Lawrence Thayer's poem, *Casey at the Bat*. They had engaged in a number of close readings by this time of the year and were accustomed to repeated reading and annotation. They also knew that their understanding of the text would unfold over several conversations with their peers.

The first pass through the text involved Mr. Taylor reading the text aloud. Mr. Taylor decided to read the text aloud because he wanted his students to get the gist of the text before exploring it in greater detail. He also knew that they would need some time to process the fact that this was more than a baseball story.

Mr. Taylor had two plans in mind for this text. First, he intended to use this text as an introduction for an essay in which students would explore the essential question, "What happens when a hero lets you down?" Second, he wanted his students to practice some of their comprehension skills, namely visualizing and inferencing, as well as their analysis skills for understanding literature. Mr. Taylor's students were not overwhelmed with the assignments. Instead, they were prepared. Their preparation rested on the close reading of complex texts that his students completed as part of their schooling experience.

When students read hard texts individually and independently and then answer questions, we do not define this as close reading. Students have to be interacting with others.

Close Reading Defined

Close reading is an instructional routine in which students are guided in their understanding of complex texts. The Aspen Institute, an educational and policy studies group with significant influence on practice, defines close reading in the following way (Brown & Kappes, 2012):

> Close Reading of text involves an investigation of a short piece of text, with multiple readings done over multiple instructional lessons. Through text-based questions and discussion, students are guided to deeply analyze and appreciate various aspects of the text, such as key vocabulary and how its meaning is shaped by context; attention to form, tone, imagery and/or rhetorical devices; the significance of word choice and syntax; and the discovery of different levels of meaning as passages are read multiple times. (p. 2)

There are a number of interrelated practices that combine to create a close reading experience. Importantly, not all texts deserve a close reading. Some texts are read for pleasure; others to find a specific bit of information. In these situations, close reading is not necessary. Close reading is also not necessary when the text is fairly accessible. In other words, close reading is typically used with complex texts— texts that do not give up their meaning easily or quickly.

Importantly, not all texts deserve a close reading.

The following salient features are necessary for students to learn to read closely (e.g., Boyles, 2013; Fisher & Frey, 2012):

- **Short, Complex Passages.** Texts selected for close reading typically range from a few paragraphs to a few pages. These texts are sufficiently complex to withstand multiple readings and challenge readers' thinking and understanding.

• **Repeated Reading.** Students reread or listen to the text, or parts of the text, for different purposes, to answer different questions, to find evidence for their inferences and conclusions, or as part of their collaborative conversations. Importantly, rereading is one of the primary scaffolds that are used during close reading. Inviting students to reread a text, looking for evidence or digging deeper into the meaning, can improve fluency and comprehension (e.g., Therrien, 2004). However, we were sensitive to the comments of Nichols, Rupley, and Rasinski (2009) who suggested that "continual reliance on repeated readings without appropriate guidance and support can lead to diminished student engagement and may not help students recognize that increased fluency provides for more focus on meaning" (p. 5). We see close reading as one type of guidance and support that harnesses the power of repeated readings.

• **Annotation.** Students in grades 3–5 write directly on the texts as they read, identifying central ideas, circling confusing words or phrases, and writing margin notes such as questions, reactions, and examples. Students in grades K–2 may or may not write directly on the texts, depending on the structure of the lesson and the difficulty of the text. Annotations can be used in narrative and informational texts, in both print and digital environments (Castek & Beach, 2013; Zywica & Gomez, 2008). Importantly, annotations serve as a scaffold, as students must slow down their reading to annotate and continue to annotate as they discuss the text with others. We have modified the recommendations of Adler and Van Doren (1940/1972) to reflect developmentally appropriate practices for elementary school students:

Students in grades 3–5 write directly on the texts as they read.

1. *Underlining* for major points.

2. *Star, asterisk, or other doodad in the margin* to be used sparingly to emphasize the ten or dozen most important statements.

3. *Numbers in the margin* to indicate a sequence of points made by the author in development of an argument.

4. *Circling of key words or phrases* to serve much the same function as underlining.

5. *Writing in the margin, or at the top or bottom of the page,* to record questions (and perhaps answers) that a passage raises in your mind (pp. 49–50).

See Figure 1.1 for a classroom poster for annotation and Figure 1.2 for a sample of a student's annotation.

- **Collaborative Conversations About the Text.** Students should interact with their peers and their teachers using academic language and argumentation skills as they discuss the text. In other words, when students read hard texts individually and independently and then answer questions, we do not define this as close reading. *Students have to be interacting with others* in such a way as to facilitate one another's understanding of the text.

Figure 1.1   Common Annotation Marks

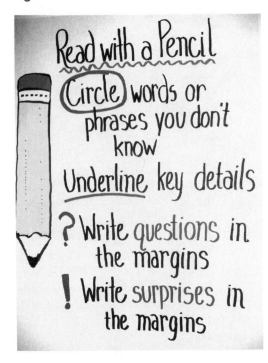

- **Text-Dependent Questions.** The majority of questions that are discussed during close reading require that students provide evidence from the text as part of their responses. The questions are not limited to recall but rather focus on various aspects of the text, including its structure, what it means, and what logical inferences can be drawn from it. As with many other aspects of close reading, the text-dependent questions serve as a scaffold for students. Teachers can ask questions strategically to focus student attention on specific aspects of the text that are challenging or confusing.

These salient features of close reading provide the scaffolds students need to understand the text. In addition, the way in which the lesson unfolds provides a scaffold for students. Close reading is not one-and-done reading. Rather, it is purposeful, careful, and thoughtful. As we have noted before, complex texts do not often give up their meaning

Figure 1.2   Student Annotation Sample

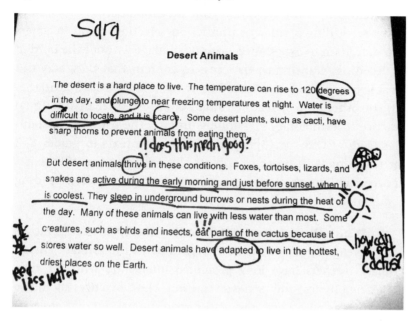

quickly or easily. Instead, readers learn to look for different things as they interact with a given text during a series of successive interactions with that text.

Close Reading in the Elementary Grades

While close reading has received quite a bit of attention in the literature (e.g., Boyles, 2013), it is important to note that close reading in the elementary grades isn't simply a watered-down version of the kind of close reading done at the secondary level. There are some important distinguishing features that align with the developmental needs of young readers (Fisher & Frey, 2012).

• **Who Is Reading?** Close reading isn't only about eyes on print; it is more accurately a means to explore the comprehension of ideas and structures more deeply. This means that teachers don't need to adhere strictly to solo, independent reading (usually interpreted as silent reading). Some texts demand to be heard and read aloud—poems, for example, as well as speeches and plays. Sometimes the teacher reads aloud (but not necessarily on the first read of the text), and other times students read aloud to their group members (but probably not on the first read of the text). The architects of the Common Core State Standards (CCSS) note that "by reading a story or nonfiction selection aloud, teachers allow children to experience written language without the burden of decoding, granting them access to content that they may not be able to read and understand by themselves" (CCSSI, 2010a, p. 28). In other words, reading aloud is an essential instructional practice in elementary classrooms. In fact, the list of text examples in the CCSS specifically identifies some texts in grades K–3 for read-alouds in order to address the cognitive gap that exists between children's listening comprehension and their reading comprehension.

> Close reading in the elementary grades is not simply a watered-down version of the kind of close reading done at the secondary level.

- **What Does Annotation Look Like?** Annotation moves on a developmental continuum, beginning in the primary grades. Primary teachers have long promoted interaction with the text, including physical and tactile interaction. These practices should be seen as steps on a path toward the more formal annotations that students in grades 3–5 (described previously) can perform. The readers at the emergent stage of literacy development draw and explain their illustrations, while an adult scribes their words on the page, a practice known as the language experience approach (Halliday, 1977). They use Wikki Stix and highlighter tape to isolate words and phrases in big books, and they witness the thinking of their teacher during modeled instruction in annotation.

- **How Is Text Used Across the Instructional Day?** Most elementary classrooms are self-contained, with students receiving instruction in language arts, mathematics, science, social studies, and the visual and performing arts from the same teacher. This lends itself beautifully to multidisciplinary examinations of texts across the day. For example, an informational text on amphibians might be introduced during the language arts block, with the initial focus on gaining a general understanding and identifying key details. Later in the day, the same text is used in the science block to explore the vocabulary and text structures used to provide an explanation of the characteristics of this animal group. The following day, during the science block, the text is used again; this time it is compared to and contrasted with a previously read book about reptiles.

The Phases of Close Reading

Close reading leads student on a cognitive path that begins with establishing the literal meaning of a text and ends with an exploration into its deeper meaning and a plan for what should occur as a result of the reading. These phases, which may roll out over several lessons, encourage students to move from surface-level comprehension to deep comprehension:

- What does the text say?

- How does the text work?

- What does the text mean?

- What does the text inspire you to do?

These phases draw on the work of other researchers, notably Adler and Van Doren (1940/1972) and Kurland (1995) and are the focus of the remainder of this book. Each of the following chapters is devoted to one of these questions. We refer to them as *phases* because they may be spread across one or more lessons, depending on how much time and discussion is needed to move students from surface-level comprehension to deep meaning. These should not be interpreted too narrowly as a recipe for a close reading lesson; rather, they should be used as a tool for organizing the journey through a piece of text.

This approach to deep comprehension instruction should also not be viewed narrowly within the language of the Common Core. As we have noted, the research on close and critical reading extends back decades. Collectively, these guiding questions provide a means for addressing close and critical reading, whether you live in a region that has adopted Common Core standards or not. While they are a method for addressing all the reading standards, they also address significant portions of the language, speaking and listening, and writing domain standards outlined in the CCSS documents (CCSSI, 2010a, 2010b). Over time, and with practice, students will ask themselves and their peers these questions as they engage with complex texts.

What Does the Text Say? The first phase concerns the literal meaning of the text, especially as it applies to explicitly stated information, as well as the central ideas or themes. Students aren't always able to determine these central themes during the first or second reading. Often, this understanding emerges more fully as the discussion progresses. The ongoing conversation in the classroom about a piece of text gives students ample opportunities to formulate and comprehend the use of language conventions and functions, especially as students in this initial phase seek to explain and give supporting evidence. These interactions with one another allow them to use talk in a variety of contexts through the communicative tasks associated with collaborative peer conversations. See Figure 1.3 for a table of intersecting anchor standards, which will be more fully explored by grade level in Chapter 2.

How Does the Text Work? A second cognitive path involves the mechanics of the piece, especially as it applies to vocabulary, the structure of the text, and the author's craft. The College and

Figure 1.3   Intersection of ELA Standards: *What Does the Text Say?*

Anchor Standards for Reading	
1	Read closely to determine what the text says explicitly and to make logical inferences from it; cite specific textual evidence when writing or speaking to support conclusions drawn from the text.
2	Determine central ideas or themes of a text and analyze their development; summarize the key supporting details and ideas.
3	Analyze how and why individuals, events, and ideas develop and interact over the course of a text.
10	Read and comprehend complex literary and informational texts independently and proficiently.

Anchor Standards for Language	
1	Demonstrate command of the conventions of standard English grammar and usage when writing or speaking.
3	Apply knowledge of language to understand how language functions in different contexts, to make effective choices for meaning or style, and to comprehend more fully when reading or listening.
6	Acquire and use accurately a range of general academic and domain-specific words and phrases sufficient for reading, writing, speaking, and listening at the college and career readiness level; demonstrate independence in gathering vocabulary knowledge when considering a word or phrase important to comprehension or expression.

Anchor Standards for Speaking and Listening	
1	Prepare for and participate effectively in a range of conversations and collaborations with diverse partners, building on others' ideas and expressing their own clearly and persuasively.
4	Present information, findings, and supporting evidence such that listeners can follow the line of reasoning and the organization, development, and style are appropriate to task, purpose, and audience.
6	Adapt speech to a variety of contexts and communicative tasks, demonstrating command of formal English when indicated or appropriate.

Career Readiness (CCR) reading **standards 4, 5,** and **6** capture the importance of zooming in at the sentence and paragraph levels. The language standards, especially CCR.L.4 and CCR.L.5, describe the essential nature of understanding figurative language, connotative meaning, and word solving. Although vocabulary is conventionally addressed early on in a reading lesson, we prefer to allow it to gestate for a bit before examining words and phrases closely. Our experience has shown us that taking time in the lesson to discuss vocabulary in the context of the reading pays off, as the overall structure of the text builds an important bridge between literal (what the text *says*) and inferential levels (what the text *means*). Figure 1.4 features a table of

Figure 1.4   Intersection of Standards: *How Does the Text Work?*

Anchor Standards for Reading	
4	Interpret words and phrases as they are used in a text, including determining technical, connotative, and figurative meanings, and analyze how specific word choices shape meaning or tone.
5	Analyze the structure of texts, including how specific sentences, paragraphs, and larger portions of the text (e.g., a section, chapter, scene, or stanza) relate to each other and the whole.
6	Assess how point of view or purpose shapes the content and style of a text.
10	Read and comprehend complex literary and informational texts independently and proficiently.

Anchor Standards for Language	
3	Apply knowledge of language to understand how language functions in different contexts, to make effective choices for meaning or style, and to comprehend more fully when reading or listening.
4	Determine or clarify the meaning of unknown and multiple-meaning words and phrases by using context clues, analyzing meaningful word parts, and consulting general and specialized reference materials, as appropriate.
5	Demonstrate understanding of figurative language, word relationships, and nuances in word meanings.
6	Acquire and use accurately a range of general academic and domain-specific words and phrases sufficient for reading, writing, speaking, and listening at the college and career readiness level; demonstrate independence in gathering vocabulary knowledge when considering a word or phrase important to comprehension or expression.

Anchor Standards for Speaking and Listening	
1	Prepare for and participate effectively in a range of conversations and collaborations with diverse partners, building on others' ideas and expressing their own clearly and persuasively.
4	Present information, findings, and supporting evidence such that listeners can follow the line of reasoning and the organization, development, and style are appropriate to task, purpose, and audience.
6	Adapt speech to a variety of contexts and communicative tasks, demonstrating command of formal English when indicated or appropriate.

intersecting anchor standards for this phase; these standards will be discussed in more detail by grade level in Chapter 3.

What Does the Text Mean? As the students' understanding of the text expands, the next cognitive path involves integrating knowledge and ideas in order to locate deeper, at times hidden, meanings and to make logical inferences based on what the text says. This speaks to some of the *qualitative* elements that make a text more complex, especially those that involve layers of meaning. Because deep meanings of texts are often subjective and speculative, debate and disagreement are more likely to occur. Properly channeled and celebrated, these alternative points of view give students the chance to evaluate other speakers' points of view and their use of rhetorical devices. In investigating *what the text means*, students focus on the author's purpose and the inferences they can make based on their understanding of the text. Students also come to understand what a text means when they analyze multiple texts on the same theme or topic. Figure 1.5 has a table of intersecting anchor standards aligned with the question of text meaning. These concepts will be revisited by grade level in Chapter 4.

What Does the Text Inspire You to Do? This final phase of close reading, which becomes more of a critical reading, is the one we find teachers are often best at, as they deeply understand the texts they are using. In fact, many of the texts we teach are ones that have inspired us in some way. However, in this case, the *you* in the question refers to the reader, who takes what has been learned from the text to create a new product.

These questions are better described as *tasks*, in that they are expressed through Socratic seminar, debates, presentations, investigations and research, tests or other assessments, and writing from sources. These tasks may involve reconsidering a previously discussed text in light of the newer one or may play a role in research or investigation. Therefore, the table in Figure 1.6 includes writing anchor standards, as many of the tasks involve informal and formal writing. These will be explored more completely by grade level in Chapter 5.

The best close readings are those that leave students with a lot of questions that they still want to answer. Often, the results of close

> Because deep meanings of texts are often subjective and speculative, debate and disagreement are more likely to occur.

Figure 1.5   Intersection of Standards: *What Does the Text Mean?*

Anchor Standards for Reading	
7	Integrate and evaluate content presented in diverse formats and media, including visually and quantitatively, as well as in words.
8	Delineate and evaluate the argument and specific claims in a text, including the validity of the reasoning as well as the relevance and sufficiency of the evidence.
9	Analyze how two or more texts address similar themes or topics in order to build knowledge or to compare the approaches the authors take.
10	Read and comprehend complex literary and informational texts independently and proficiently.
Anchor Standards for Language	
1	Demonstrate command of the conventions of standard English grammar and usage when writing or speaking.
3	Apply knowledge of language to understand how language functions in different contexts, to make effective choices for meaning or style, and to comprehend more fully when reading or listening.
6	Acquire and use accurately a range of general academic and domain-specific words and phrases sufficient for reading, writing, speaking, and listening at the college and career readiness level; demonstrate independence in gathering vocabulary knowledge when considering a word or phrase important to comprehension or expression.
Anchor Standards for Speaking and Listening	
1	Prepare for and participate effectively in a range of conversations and collaborations with diverse partners, building on others' ideas and expressing their own clearly and persuasively.
2	Integrate and evaluate information presented in diverse media and formats, including visually, quantitatively, and orally.
3	Evaluate a speaker's point of view, reasoning, and use of evidence and rhetoric.
4	Present information, findings, and supporting evidence such that listeners can follow the line of reasoning and the organization, development, and style are appropriate to task, purpose, and audience.
6	Adapt speech to a variety of contexts and communicative tasks, demonstrating command of formal English when indicated or appropriate.

reading are teacher-directed or shared research as students are inspired to find the answers to their own questions.

How Much Frontloading Is Too Much (or Not Enough)?

The Bard never said, "To frontload or not to frontload, that is the question," but we, like Hamlet, are faced with a dilemma, and ours is causing all of us to re-examine this instructional practice. And

Figure 1.6   Intersection of Standards: *What Does the Text Inspire You to Do?*

Anchor Standards for Reading

7	Integrate and evaluate content presented in diverse formats and media, including visually and quantitatively, as well as in words.
8	Delineate and evaluate the argument and specific claims in a text, including the validity of the reasoning as well as the relevance and sufficiency of the evidence.
9	Analyze how two or more texts address similar themes or topics in order to build knowledge or to compare the approaches the authors take.
10	Read and comprehend complex literary and informational texts independently and proficiently.

Anchor Standards for Language

1	Demonstrate command of the conventions of standard English grammar and usage when writing or speaking.
2	Demonstrate command of the conventions of standard English capitalization, punctuation, and spelling when writing.
3	Apply knowledge of language to understand how language functions in different contexts, to make effective choices for meaning or style, and to comprehend more fully when reading or listening.
6	Acquire and use accurately a range of general academic and domain-specific words and phrases sufficient for reading, writing, speaking, and listening at the college and career readiness level; demonstrate independence in gathering vocabulary knowledge when considering a word or phrase important to comprehension or expression.

Anchor Standards for Speaking and Listening

1	Prepare for and participate effectively in a range of conversations and collaborations with diverse partners, building on others' ideas and expressing their own clearly and persuasively.
2	Integrate and evaluate information presented in diverse media and formats, including visually, quantitatively, and orally.
3	Evaluate a speaker's point of view, reasoning, and use of evidence and rhetoric.
4	Present information, findings, and supporting evidence such that listeners can follow the line of reasoning and the organization, development, and style are appropriate to task, purpose, and audience.
6	Adapt speech to a variety of contexts and communicative tasks, demonstrating command of formal English when indicated or appropriate.

Anchor Standards for Writing

1	Write arguments to support claims in an analysis of substantive topics or texts, using valid reasoning and relevant and sufficient evidence.
2	Write informative/explanatory texts to examine and convey complex ideas and information clearly and accurately through the effective selection, organization, and analysis of content.
3	Write narratives to develop real or imagined experiences or events using effective technique, well-chosen details, and well-structured event sequences.
7	Conduct short as well as more sustained research projects based on focused questions, demonstrating understanding of the subject under investigation.
8	Gather relevant information from multiple print and digital sources, assess the credibility and accuracy of each source, and integrate the information while avoiding plagiarism.
9	Draw evidence from literary or informational texts to support analysis, reflection, and research.

that's a good thing, by the way. As educators, we must be willing to question longstanding assumptions about our practices in light of new information. Isn't that what critical literacy (which we actively encourage in our students) is all about?

Of growing concern is that the general approach of dismantling any and all obstacles that are in a reader's way diminishes the opportunity to resolve problems. In other words, we need to thoughtfully and intentionally allow for problems to emerge, so students can attempt to work them out. This can pose a challenge for well-meaning teachers who have used a preteaching approach that frontloads the main points of the text in advance of the reading. There's logic in doing so: The less time devoted to discussion of the text, the more likely it is that students will require some frontloading. In other words, if it's a "one-and-done" text, then more frontloading is going to be required.

In addition, the characteristics of the learner at times necessitate frontloading. For example, a student who is new to the language of instruction is likely to require more frontloading. Others may have limited background knowledge that is going to significantly impact their ability to integrate new knowledge. But to remove *all* struggle from a reader's path also removes the need to deploy the strategies we've been teaching them. Imagine a medical student's education that included an exhaustive list of diseases and their treatments, but no experience at applying this knowledge with real patients in real time. In a similar way, students learn about what to do when comprehension breaks down. But if readers have little classroom experience in regaining understanding of a text, they are not going to do so on their own when reading independently. This in turn can stall their growth in accessing increasingly complex text. When they are doing close reading, students can practice and apply their problem-solving skills. And resolving problems builds stamina, persistence, and confidence. But we also don't want students to quit in frustration, or avoid more challenging pieces in favor of the comfort zone. We have no problem with students selecting texts that are in their comfort zone, especially for independent reading, but that zone should expand over the course of the year.

It is important to recognize that scaffolded instruction doesn't happen only in advance of the reading. It also occurs *during* the reading

> Of growing concern is that the general approach of dismantling any and all obstacles that are in a reader's way diminishes the opportunity to resolve problems.

and rereading of a text. The characteristics of a close reading discussed earlier are important precisely because they are *distributed* scaffolds, rather than frontloaded ones. Rereading, with guidance, provides students with the time to soak in information. Collaborative conversations with peers provide a means for students to clarify and consolidate. The habit of annotation ("reading with a pencil") slows down the reading process so that students can understand the text more deeply. Newkirk (2012) writes

> To read slowly is to maintain an intimate relationship with a writer. If we are to respond to a writer, we must be *responsible*. We commit ourselves to follow a train of thought, to mentally construct characters, to follow the unfolding of an idea, to hear a text, to attend to language, to question, to visualize scenes. It means paying attention to the decisions a writer makes. (p. 2)

In addition to the three aforementioned distributed scaffolds (multiple readings, collaborative conversations, annotations), there is a fourth: thoughtfully planned text-dependent questions. These questions move students from literal to inferential and critical levels of meaning, both within a single book or article and across multiple texts.

Resolving problems builds stamina, persistence, and confidence. But we also don't want students to quit in frustration, or avoid more challenging pieces in favor of the comfort zone.

The Distributed Scaffolds of Close Reading

1. Multiple Readings
2. Collaborative Conversations
3. Annotations
4. Thoughtfully Planned Text-Dependent Questions

Text-Dependent Questions Drive Close Reading

This last point is the focus of this book. The questions teachers and students ask about a text serve not only as a scaffold for learning but also as a main driver of close reading itself. These questions frame the extended discussion of a text and invite children to coconstruct knowledge in the company of their teacher. These questions advance students through a process of more deeply understanding a text.

Let's look at the phases again, more closely examining the question *types* in each phase, and let's look at examples of questions that Mr. Taylor used with his fourth grade class.

Phase 1: What Does the Text *Say*?

General understanding questions cause students to attend to the major points in the text, such as the sequence of events, the story arc or important plot points, or the main claim and the evidence furnished. These are paired with *key detail questions* that drill down further, especially in exploring the relationship between the main ideas and the supporting details. These are often phrased as *who, what, when, where, why, how much,* or *how many* kinds of questions. The purpose of these key detail questions is not to quiz students on minutia, but rather to link the major idea of the piece to the details the author has furnished that directly support it.

> The characteristics of a close reading discussed earlier are important precisely because they are *distributed* scaffolds, rather than frontloaded ones.

In his lesson with the fourth graders that opened this chapter, Mr. Taylor posed several text-dependent questions that built his students' foundational knowledge about what the text said. Therefore, his initial general understanding and key detail questions invited students to identify the main message:

- *Who is Casey?*

- *Where does the story take place?*

- *Who is telling the story?*

- *Describe Casey's character traits.*

- *How do you know the crowd is excited Casey's at bat?*

- *How was Casey feeling about the umpire calling strikes? How do you know?*

Phase 2: How Does the Text *Work*?

The next category of text-dependent questions involves the mechanics of the text. Questions about *vocabulary words and phrases* are essential because they provide students with opportunities to resolve the unknown. Such questions may be directed to the denotative meaning by prompting students to use their structural and contextual analysis skills. Importantly, they can also include questions about the connotations of the word or phrase, including word relationships, idioms, adages, similes, and metaphors. Going deeper still, *text structure questions* ask students to locate the ways in which cause and effect, problem–solution, compare–contrast, temporal order, or extended description are used by the writer to maintain a logical flow in an expository piece. Within narrative text types, structures include story grammar, chapters, scenes, and stanzas. Poetic forms are also explored, and such devices include rhyme, meter, alliteration, and onomatopoeia. Vocabulary plays an important role here as well, especially in connecting signal and transitional words and phrases to the structures utilized. Text structure questions do not just zoom in on a few sentences. Text structures also unfold across paragraphs and passages, especially as they forward a plot, an explanation, or an opinion. Therefore, questions that cause students to apply literary analysis (e.g., of characterization, narration, and point of view) give students a chance to see text structures at play over a longer piece of text.

Finally, *author's craft questions* cause students to notice the writer's deliberate use of word choice, syntax, dialogue, and epilogues, and choice of genre to shape the message. These may include the ways in which the author uses text features such as illustrations, diagrams, and captions to convey information. For primary readers, answering these questions involves knowing about covers and title pages as well as text features such as headings and glossaries. In his close reading of *Casey at the Bat*, Mr. Taylor returned his fourth grade students to an examination of the structures used in the text:

- *What does the author mean by the phrase, "Cooney died at first, and Barrows did the same"?*

- *What does the word* stood *mean in the phrase, "The score stood 4 to 2"?*

- *What makes this poem a narrative?*

- *The poet says "10,000 eyes were on him. . . ." How many people would that be in the stands? Is this hyperbole, or is it accurate?*

- *How does the mood shift from the beginning of the poem to the end?*

During close reading lessons in the intermediate grades, we discourage children from always raising their hands and waiting to be called on, as it makes us feel like traffic cops. We encourage them to speak directly to one another, not solely to us.

- *How does the figurative language help the reader visualize the hidden meaning?*

- *How does the author help us understand what "doffed his hat" means?*

- *How do the audience's "tongues applaud"?*

Phase 3: What Does the Text *Mean*?

Are you tracing the trajectory of the questions? We began with discussion of the literal-level meaning of the text (general understanding and key detail questions), and then moved to examining the mechanics of the piece (vocabulary, text structure, and author's craft). This forms a solid foundation for the next category of questions, which involve the deep meaning of a text. In Phase 3, *author's purpose questions* probe the stated and hidden or subversive intentions of the author (but not all authors have such intentions) and the relationship the author has to the topic, especially questioning the author's credibility and expertise. Students in the elementary grades explore the author's use of reason and evidence to support information or opinions. Questions that invite *intertextual connections* foster the habit of thinking across texts to compare, contrast, and consider how different writers address similar themes and subjects.

Although vocabulary is conventionally addressed early on in a reading lesson, we prefer to allow it to gestate for a bit before examining words and phrases closely.

The text-dependent questions Mr. Taylor posed to his fourth grade students moved them toward deeper understanding:

- *The character of Casey tells us a little bit about the difference between being confident and being too confident. Was Casey too confident? Why? What happened?*

- *What is the author saying about Flynn and Blake?*

- *Why does the author say, "The band is playing somewhere . . . but there is no joy tonight in Mudville"?*

- *What is the author's message? What does this all mean, really?*

Phase 4: What Does the Text *Inspire You to Do*?

A final category of questions is reserved for encouraging students to move beyond the text at hand by taking action. These questions invite *opinion with evidence* and result in some task. They invite students to take a critical stance by examining power structures, considering alternate perspectives, and posing problems themselves that lead to action (McLaughlin & DeVoogd, 2004). Such questions lead to teacher-directed or shared research or investigation, and are expressed through debate, presentations, or writing. In other words, students use the text as a platform for what will occur next. You'll recall from the opening scenario that Mr. Taylor had two tasks in mind for his fourth grade students. The first was to compose a response to the following prompt:

> *What happens when a hero lets you down? After reading the poem, write a response to the essential question in which you analyze the perspective of others. Be sure to use at least four examples from the text or other texts in order to support your position.*

The progression of text-dependent questions used by Mr. Taylor and others featured throughout this book provide an added benefit, in that they afford teachers ongoing opportunities to check for understanding, make formative assessment decisions, and ensure that students engage in critical thinking. The Depth of Knowledge (DOK) framework (Webb, 2002) is a widely used method for gauging the rigor of thinking necessary to successfully perform a task. The four cognitive levels described in the framework are as follows:

Level 1: Recall and Recognition tasks

Level 2: Skills and Concepts tasks

Level 3: Strategic Thinking and Reasoning tasks

Level 4: Extended Thinking tasks

The DOK is used, for instance, to determine whether assessment questions address the full range of critical thinking. In addition, it is used to align instructional practices and curricular materials. The range of text-dependent questions described throughout this book have been developed to aid teachers in moving students systematically across a continuum of increasing complexity. Figure 1.7 further describes the relationship between DOK and text-dependent questions.

These questions invite *opinion with evidence* and result in some task.

Figure 1.7   **Relationship Between Depth of Knowledge and Types of Text-Dependent Questions**

	Level 1 (Recall)	Level 2 (Skill/Concept)	Level 3 (Strategic Thinking)	Level 4 (Extended Thinking)
General Understanding *What does the text say?*	Identify sequence of events, major plot points, story arc, or main claim and evidence furnished.			
Key Details *What does the text say?*	Answer questions about information provided directly in the text (i.e., who, what, when, where, why, how much, or how many).	Determine importance of ideas, link main idea to supporting details.		
Vocabulary *How does the text work?*		Identify denotation: Use structural and contextual analysis to resolve meaning.	Identify connotation and shades of meaning, figurative language and analogies; interpret mood and tone.	
Structure *How does the text work?*		Locate text structures (cause and effect, problem and solution, description, chronological order).	Link major concepts or ideas across paragraphs and passages; interpret elements of text using literary analysis (e.g., characterization, point of view, narration).	
Author's Craft *How does the text work?*			Identify the ways a writer's decisions about word choice and text structures serve to convey experiences, information, or arguments.	
Author's Purpose *What does the text mean?*		Locate stated purpose of the text, if applicable; analyze author's relationship to the content of the piece.	Determine hidden or subversive intentions and hypothesize possible motivations or interests.	Critique author's purpose using rhetorical structures and formal reasoning; link these to historical, sociological, or psychological phenomena.

(Continued)

Figure 1.7   (Continued)

	Level 1 (Recall)	Level 2 (Skill/Concept)	Level 3 (Strategic Thinking)	Level 4 (Extended Thinking)
Intertextual Connections *What does the text mean?*				Compare and contrast information or viewpoints across multiple texts.
Opinion With Evidence or Argument *What does the text inspire you to do?*			Identify missing or incomplete information that merits further investigation.	Construct formal original arguments using textual evidence; reflect on the role of one's own biases in interpreting the text; formulate a plan of action or next steps for investigation or research.

Source: Adapted from Norman Webb's Depth of Knowledge Chart © 2002 and Types of Text Dependent Questions Chart, Fisher & Frey © IRA 2012.

Use Text-Dependent Questions Judiciously

Effective text-dependent questions are the product of the teacher's close reading of the text. This in itself is a habit to build, as many of us are more accustomed to examining the content (that is, the literal level of the text) without going much further. That means that we have to allow ourselves a bit more time to sit with a piece of text we've selected for a close reading in order to locate the structural and inferential levels of meaning. If you're having trouble in doing so, even after time spent reading closely, then perhaps the selection isn't a good choice for a close reading, as it may not be "juicy" enough to warrant that level of attention.

Resist the urge to turn close reading into an independent activity. The point of a close reading is to foster extended discussions about a piece of text, so that the group can coconstruct the meaning. Close reading is social learning at its best. That means that it is critical for the teacher to listen attentively to what is being discussed. After the initial literal meaning of the text has been established, many text-dependent questions raise insights and observations by children that will surprise you. Be prepared for that. Watch the line of thinking develop across the group, and allow them the time to process their ideas. Text-dependent questions are not about waiting for one student to utter the correct reply and then moving on. They're about dialogic teaching, where "teachers and students act as co-inquirers, collaboratively engaging in a generation and evaluation of new interpretations of texts" (Reznitskaya, 2012, p. 446). Students are encouraged to elaborate on answers, teachers

The point of a close reading is to foster extended discussions about a piece of text, so that the group can coconstruct the meaning.

monitor their conversational moves to keep the discussion moving forward, and all group members (not just the teacher) monitor and maintain the flow of the conversation (Reznitskaya, 2012). During close reading lessons in the intermediate grades, we discourage children from always raising their hands and waiting to be called on, as it makes us feel like traffic cops. We encourage them to speak directly to one another, not solely to us. And we encourage them to ask their own questions, about the text and what it means to them.

Listening attentively means that some of the text-dependent questions you carefully prepared might not get used. In many cases, the thinking you hoped to provoke in your students through one question is addressed in the discussion of another. That's what often happens. The purpose of these questions is to build the habit of thinking critically, and because of this, the cognitive path students set out on isn't always predictable. We develop these text-dependent questions to keep in our back pocket, so to speak. We'd rather have them available, but never used, than fail to unearth an important point that is essential to students' deeper understanding.

Be prepared for the close reading lessons you've crafted to take a different period of time than you have expected. Some are shorter, in that students move more quickly through a discussion of a text than you had expected. More often, they will stall at a point you had not anticipated. "I taught them this already.

They should know this," you'll think. When they hesitate and struggle, view it properly as an indication that you are provoking deeper thinking. That's exactly what you want to achieve in a close reading lesson. You are building the habit of reading closely and interrogating the text. Don't expect that all these text-dependent questions will be addressed in one lesson. We teach at the high school level, and our close reading lessons are typically 45 minutes or an hour long. Often, close reading lessons extend over two or three periods. In other words, we return to the same piece of text but with a different intent. Sometimes we work with other teachers to use an interdisciplinary approach, such as examining a speech in English class for its rhetorical structures and in history class for its political context and implications.

QUESTION •YOURSELF

Close reading of complex texts builds a habit for students, a habit that will serve them well throughout their lives. As is true for all habits, good and bad, an investment of time is required. When a group of researchers examined the time it took for people to develop fairly simple habits (self-selected ones such as drinking more water each day or doing sit-ups before breakfast), they found that the average number of repetitions required was 66 before the person reached a plateau (Lally, van Jaarsveld, Potts, & Wardle, 2010). Interestingly, some people developed a habit in 18 days, whereas others took 254 days. These researchers noted that

- Missing a single day did not reduce the chance of forming a habit.

- A subgroup took much longer than the others to form their habits, perhaps suggesting some people are habit resistant.

- Other types of more complex habits may well take much longer.

What does that mean for us? For one thing, children aren't likely to develop the habit of reading closely very quickly. It will take time and practice. For another, there may be some students who develop this habit quickly and others who need more time and support to do so. Unlike learning to eat a piece of fruit each day or walking for 15 minutes, which were some of the habits people in the study decided to develop, reading closely is a complex cognitive process and not a relatively simple behavior. To complicate this further, we intentionally raise the complexity of the text with which students are trying to develop this habit. We say this to provide some reassurance that the effort does pay off, eventually. At first, children will require a lot of guidance and support. Over time, they assume increased responsibility for their discussions about complex texts. We know that they have developed this habit when they begin asking each other the type of questions outlined in this book, because they have heard us use them so often and have become used to thinking about texts in these ways. And it's pretty rewarding when a group of children meets to talk about a complex piece of text, slowly and intentionally uncovering the big ideas and comparing those ideas to their own, expanding their understanding of the world around them.

Videos

To read a QR code, you must have a smartphone or tablet with a camera. We recommend that you download a QR code reader app that is made specifically for your phone or tablet brand.

Videos can also be accessed at
www.corwin.com/textdependentquestions

Video 1.1 Doug Fisher and Nancy Frey reveal how repeated reading and collaborative conversation can give students the opportunity to acquire new knowledge.

Video 1.2 Several teachers discuss the importance of collaborating with other instructors to provide a range of texts that can help students acquire different skills.

Video 1.3 Teachers give insight into bringing excitement back into the classroom—both for the students and the instructors.

Video 1.4 A successful classroom is full of students who are willing and able to engage, but they need a teacher to lead them in their learning.

2

WHAT DOES
THE TEXT **SAY**?

The habit of reading closely begins with inspection. Inspections of facilities, products, and services all rely on formal processes. As citizens, we count on inspectors to keep our food chain safe and our transportation systems running smoothly. These inspectors are trained experts who are knowledgeable about what they are inspecting, and they begin by taking a measure of the characteristics of the item under consideration. What they select to measure is not the product of convenience; inspectors know what they are looking for and seek specific information in order to gauge quality and estimate the nature of what they are inspecting.

Close reading helps students become, in part, text inspectors. Developing the skill of inspection requires expertise: knowing what to look for. Elementary readers are not experts; in fact, they are at the beginning stages of developing the ability to take the measure of a text in order to understand its characteristics. And they need guidance in how to do so. Unfortunately, sometimes young readers are simply told what is important and are not given a chance to develop the skills to inspect a text on their own. This leaves them sorely lacking in their ability to inspect a text when not in the company of the teacher. But how can we help our students build these skills?

Text-dependent questions point students to the elements of a complex text so that they can gather useful information. Targeted questioning is crucial, because it serves to focus their attention on important parts of the text without telling them what the text says. Like any good inspector-in-training, students build the habit of detecting clues—as well as spotting and resolving problems—when they have frequent practice and when they receive feedback about their efforts. But the key to a good inspection is in knowing where to look and what to look for. The text-dependent questions designed for use during early readings of a text provide students with a model of inspection they internalize over time. In this chapter, we focus on the first phase of inquiry: understanding *what the text says*.

An Invitation to Read Closely: *Literal*-Level Questions

Although frequently maligned, questions about the ideas and concepts directly stated in the text set the stage for deeper understanding. To be sure, it is a problem when the questions posed to readers fail to progress beyond explicit meaning. But understanding the literal level of a text is the gateway to analysis and conceptual thinking. Adler and Van Doren (1940/1972) noted that the first two of the four questions readers pose to themselves focus on determining the gist and identifying the details. In their words,

"What is the book about as a whole?"

"What is being said in detail, and how?"

"Is it true, as a whole or in part?"

"What of it?" (pp. 46–47)

But they caution that readers' ability to address the last two questions is predicated on having satisfactorily answered the first two,

---

Although frequently maligned, questions about the ideas and concepts directly stated in the text set the stage for deeper understanding.

noting that "you have to know what is being said before you can decide whether it is true or not" (p. 47). Adler and Van Doren were concerned with the questions readers ask themselves. In this book, we focus on questions that teachers and children ask related to complex text such that collaborative conversations and deeper meaning result.

Why Students Need This Type of Questioning

Posing questions that invite students to locate a sequence of events, the major plot points, or the arc of a story assists them in gaining a general understanding of a text. Some students do this automatically, while others benefit from lingering on these types of questions. When the text is complex enough, students will need to think about their general understanding and the details. On the other hand, when readers read texts that are easier for them, there is often no need to start with these types of questions. In other words, these questions serve as a scaffold for students to access complex texts. That's not to say that they won't also get some deeper meanings on their initial reading of the text, but rather that teachers can use this line of questioning to check for understanding. Over time, this habit translates into students having a bit more persistence with a difficult piece of text—and hopefully into a stronger belief in themselves as capable learners.

> The probing question that follows the initial question makes all the difference. These probes invite students to furnish evidence to support their answers.

Questions about the explicit meaning of the text are also beneficial for struggling readers. The probing question that follows the initial question makes all the difference. These probes invite students to furnish evidence to support their answers. Consider the learning effects of two different questioning cycles in a second grade science class:

> **Ms. Jeffers:** *We just read to two paragraphs that described soil. What's in soil?*
>
> **William:** There's rocks, and there's plants, and there's water.
>
> **Ms. Jeffers:** Good! *So is soil a living thing?*

The students in the science class who read and understood the content of the text were able to follow this line of questioning. But those who had a shakier grasp of the reading were still trying to figure out how their classmates knew the answer. A follow-up probe asking for evidence untangled some confusion for these readers:

> **Ms. Jeffers:** *We just read two paragraphs that described soil. What's in soil?*
>
> **William:** There's rocks, and there's plants, and there's water.
>
> **Ms. Jeffers:** *Can you tell us where you found that information? I'd like everyone else to look as well.*
>
> **William:** [after searching for a few moments] It's in the first paragraph. There's a sentence that says, "Soil is made of rocks, water, air, and plants that used to be alive."
>
> **Ms. Jeffers:** *Does everyone see that? I'd like for you to underline those words. But now I have another question. Does that mean that soil is alive?*
>
> **Roldolfo (a struggling reader):** It's in the next sentence. Right here is says: "Soil isn't alive, even though it has plants in it."

The follow-up probe in the second example slowed down the instruction enough to allow others to catch up. The added voice of another student expanded the conversation from a single exchange with an individual to one involving another learner. As well, the direction to the entire class to look in the text and annotate it invited fuller participation and transformed the learning environment from a passive experience to an active one.

But what about those students who can already locate this information? Doesn't dwelling on literal-level questions bore them? We argue no, because the probe is asking them to do what many of them are not accustomed to doing, which is citing textual evidence. In the language of the Common Core State Standards (CCSS), students are expected to "cite specific evidence when offering an oral or written interpretation of a text . . . to use relevant evidence when supporting their own points in writing and speaking, making their reasoning clear to the reader or listener" (CCSSI, 2010a, p. 7). By the end of second grade, they're asking and answering questions about the key details of the text, especially questions that ask about *who*, *what, when, where,* and *how.* Whether you are in a state or territory that is directly tied to the Common Core standards or not, citing and using supporting evidence to support your points is a critical skill. As students progress through the elementary grades, they should be able to use text to support their answers. Even in conversation, a speaker is required to provide evidence. The ability to do so is a skill and a habit. By requesting that students supply such evidence in discussion, we build both.

Teaching students how to use evidence to support your point is critical.

In our experience, children catch on quickly to this procedure. Students who are consistently asked to provide evidence begin furnishing evidence on their own without prompting. They point out an important phrase or sentence in a passage as they reply to a query—"At the top of page 36, in the second sentence, it says. . . ." Younger students will point to an element in an illustration and say, "See how the cat is peeking around the corner of the door? That's how I know he's trying to sneak up on the mouse." In turn, their annotation skills improve as they start anticipating what will be asked of them. They mark up the text and enumerate examples and arguments. And in the meantime, students who struggle get better at locating and attending to key details, because they hear the explanations of others concerning the location of this information and begin to explain it themselves.

But students who read at and above grade level benefit from the development of this habit as well. We've encountered students who are reaching the outer limits of their ability to glean facts from a text and are now confronting unfamiliar challenges as they read more complex ones. Some of the more basic comprehension approaches that were sufficient for them as early readers are now beginning to fail them. Even among those who are still going strong, few are adept at utilizing evidence from texts in their writing. In particular, they lack the ability to select the phrases and sentences that best support their opinions. Routinely requiring students to supply evidence about the text builds this skill. Over time, skill becomes habit.

Why Classroom Discussion Is Crucial

The positive effects gained by attention to the general meaning of the text and the key details of the text are muted, if not entirely undone, if we ask children to do this work in silence, as an independent activity. Turn to the back of any school textbook, and you'll find questions derived directly from the text. Yet telling students to read the chapter and then answer the questions at the end of it doesn't result in much learning. At best it is a recognition and recall task. What's missing? In a word, discussion.

Classroom discussions allow for the coconstruction of knowledge. Discussion elevates the act of reading deeply from a private one to a public one. But dialogic teaching—that is, teaching through discussion—is not an endless round of Q and A. It is also not telling children what the text is about as a frontload, before they've ever read the text. As we noted in Chapter 1, simply telling students what they should think and know is insufficient and ineffective. In fact, it breeds dependency, as students come to rely on the teacher, and not themselves, as the interpreter of text. Isabel Beck and Margaret McKeown (2001) developed the practice of Text Talk for use during interactive read-alouds to ensure that students develop the skills necessary to comprehend complex texts:

- Select texts that are intellectually challenging.

- Design initial questions that ask students to explain ideas rather than simply recall facts.

- Ask follow-up questions to encourage elaboration.

- Reserve discussion about illustrations until later, when the meaning of the text is becoming clearer.

- Solicit background knowledge carefully, and in service of understanding the meaning of the story; do not allow students simply to recount individual experiences.

> The positive effects gained by attention to the general meaning of the text and the key details of the text are muted, if not entirely undone, if we ask children to do this work in silence, as an independent activity.

- Delay vocabulary discussions until later, after some initial meaning of the text has been understood.

Primary readers are vulnerable to developing habits that cause them to attend to other elements rather than the information in the text itself. Beck and McKeown (2001) note that kindergarten and first grade students in read-alouds will pay more attention to the illustrations and their own background knowledge than to what has been presented in the text itself.

Wilkerson and Son (2011) reviewed studies focused on dialogic teaching, including those focused on such well-known approaches as Question the Author (Beck, McKeown, Hamilton, & Kucan, 1997), Paideia Seminars (Billings & Fitzgerald, 2002), and Grand Conversations (Eeds & Wells, 1989). Although each differs in terms of its philosophical roots—Question the Author owes a debt of gratitude to Vygotsky, Grand Conversations are grounded in the work of Louise Rosenblatt, and Paideia Seminars are based on Socratic talk—all were effective at deepening conversation. However, Wilkerson and Son caution "that the success of discussion hinges not on increasing the amount of student talk per se, but in enhancing the quality of the talk" (p. 371).

> Simply telling students what they should think and know is insufficient and ineffective. In fact, it breeds dependency.

Questions focused on the literal level of meaning of a text will not foster the kind of critical thinking we seek from our students. But they are the start of the journey. To put it plainly, students must have a solid foundation of understanding about *what the text says* before they can get to *what the text means*. We do not view this as a bottom-up approach to comprehension. While we discuss the development of text-dependent questions in a linear fashion, in practice we often find ourselves deploying them in a more iterative fashion. For example, a discussion focused on deeper meaning, say on an author's hidden purpose for writing a piece, may loop back to a reexamination of the definition of an overlooked term. An exploration of the logical inferences that can be made from a text may require further analysis of the details from the text. Having said that, we recognize that conversations about complex text begin with text-dependent questions designed to clarify the general understanding of a text and the key details we'll need to determine exactly *what the text says*.

How Examining *What the Text Says* Addresses the STANDARDS

Learning from, talking about, and composing texts are at the heart of the Common Core State Standards. Text-based discussions teach students how to approach, analyze, and evaluate texts. In addition, regular exposure to and discussion of complex texts provides students with extensive practice in looking at what authors do to convey experience, inform and explain, and formulate reasoned arguments. While this book is not about writing, it should be noted that young writers are, in part, apprenticed into composition through discussions of mentor texts. As is noted on the webpage for Gallagher (2011), "If you want to learn how to shoot a basketball, you begin by carefully observing someone who knows how to shoot a basketball. If you want to be a writer, you begin by carefully observing the work of accomplished writers" (www.stenhouse.com/html/write-like-this.htm). As students read and discuss complex texts, they begin to approximate this type of writing and thinking into their own creations.

Discussions framed by text-dependent questions allow teachers to address standards in reading and language as well as in speaking and listening. These domains don't exist in isolation from one another. As we read, we marshal what we know about language. As we discuss a text, we enact our speaking and listening skills to understand and be understood. The concise nature of the standards is a signal to us that a given lesson is likely to teach toward standards that traverse the domains. In focusing first on *what the text says*, students acquire skills and habits in reading, language, speaking, and listening.

Reading Standards

The first cognitive path, to determine *what the text says*, is described in **reading standards 1, 2, 3,** and **10. Standards 1** ("read closely") and **10** ("complex texts") bookend the comprehension standards listed in between. **Standard 1** uses the same language for asking and answering questions about key details in literature and informational texts. As discussed previously, the prompts used as a follow-up to text-dependent questions build students' habit, over time, of citing textual evidence, which in turn makes it more likely that they will provide evidence in their writing, not just in their discussions. Text-dependent questions that focus on the general understanding of a text help children locate the main topic or main idea, and key detail questions cause them to examine the ways in which these items relate to the overall meaning, described as the central message, lesson, or moral in the lower grades **(standard 2).** In grades 4 and 5, the focus moves to locating the theme. Taken together, these details are necessary not only to provide the foundation for drawing inferences; they are also critical for constructing an accurate summary. Figure 2.1 provides an overview of the standards that focus on *what the text says*.

Figure 2.1   Reading Standards That Focus on *What the Text Says*

Standard (Grade)	Literary	Informational
1 (K)	With prompting and support, ask and answer questions about key details in a text.	
1 (1)	Ask and answer questions about key details in a text.	
1 (2)	Ask and answer such questions as *who, what, where, when, why,* and *how* to demonstrate understanding of key details in a text.	
1 (3)	Ask and answer questions to demonstrate understanding of a text, referring explicitly to the text as the basis for the answers.	
1 (4)	Refer to details and examples in a text when explaining what the text says explicitly and when drawing inferences from the text.	
1 (5)	Quote accurately from a text when explaining what the text says explicitly and when drawing inferences from the text.	
2 (K)	With prompting and support, retell familiar stories, including key details.	With prompting and support, identify the main topic and retell key details of a text.
2 (1)	Retell stories, including key details, and demonstrate understanding of their central message or lesson.	Identify the main topic and retell key details of a text.
2 (2)	Recount stories, including fables and folktales from diverse cultures, and determine their central message, lesson, or moral.	Identify the main topic of a multiparagraph text as well as the focus of specific paragraphs within the text.
2 (3)	Recount stories, including fables, folktales, and myths from diverse cultures; determine the central message, lesson, or moral and explain how it is conveyed through key details in the text.	Determine the main idea of a text; recount the key details and explain how they support the main idea.
2 (4)	Determine a theme of a story, drama, or poem from details in the text; summarize the text.	Determine the main idea of a text and explain how it is supported by key details; summarize the text.
2 (5)	Determine a theme of a story, drama, or poem from details in the text, including how characters in a story or drama respond to challenges or how the speaker in a poem reflects upon a topic; summarize the text.	Determine two or more main ideas of a text and explain how they are supported by key details; summarize the text.
3 (K)	With prompting and support, identify characters, settings, and major events in a story.	With prompting and support, describe the connection between two individuals, events, ideas, or pieces of information in a text.
3 (1)	Describe characters, settings, and major events in a story, using key details.	Describe the connection between two individuals, events, ideas, or pieces of information in a text.

(Continued)

Figure 2.1 (Continued)

Standard (Grade)	Literary	Informational
3 (2)	Describe how characters in a story respond to major events and challenges.	Describe the connection between a series of historical events, scientific ideas or concepts, or steps in technical procedures in a text.
3 (3)	Describe characters in a story (e.g., their traits, motivations, or feelings) and explain how their actions contribute to the sequence of events.	Describe the relationship between a series of historical events, scientific ideas or concepts, or steps in technical procedures in a text, using language that pertains to time, sequence, and cause/effect.
3 (4)	Describe in depth a character, setting, or event in a story or drama, drawing on specific details in the text (e.g., a character's thoughts, words, or actions).	Explain events, procedures, ideas, or concepts in a historical, scientific, or technical text, including what happened and why, based on specific information in the text.
3 (5)	Compare and contrast two or more characters, settings, or events in a story or drama, drawing on specific details in the text (e.g., how characters interact).	Explain the relationships or interactions between two or more individuals, events, ideas, or concepts in a historical, scientific, or technical text based on specific information in the text.
10 (K)	Actively engage in group reading activities with purpose and understanding.	
10 (1)	With prompting and support, read prose and poetry of appropriate complexity for grade 1.	With prompting and support, read informational texts appropriately complex for grade 1.
10 (2)	By the end of the year, read and comprehend literature, including stories and poetry, in the grades 2–3 text complexity band proficiently, with scaffolding as needed at the high end of the range.	By the end of year, read and comprehend informational texts, including history/social studies, science, and technical texts, in the grades 2–3 text complexity band proficiently, with scaffolding as needed at the high end of the range.
10 (3)	By the end of the year, read and comprehend literature, including stories, dramas, and poetry, at the high end of the grades 2–3 text complexity band independently and proficiently.	By the end of the year, read and comprehend informational texts, including history/social studies, science, and technical texts, at the high end of the grades 2–3 text complexity band independently and proficiently.
10 (4)	By the end of the year, read and comprehend literature, including stories, dramas, and poetry, in the grades 4–5 text complexity band proficiently, with scaffolding as needed at the high end of the range.	By the end of year, read and comprehend informational texts, including history/social studies, science, and technical texts, in the grades 4–5 text complexity band proficiently, with scaffolding as needed at the high end of the range.
10 (5)	By the end of the year, read and comprehend literature, including stories, dramas, and poetry, at the high end of the grades 4–5 text complexity band independently and proficiently.	By the end of the year, read and comprehend informational texts, including history/social studies, science, and technical texts, at the high end of the grades 4–5 text complexity band independently and proficiently.

Another facet important to understanding *what the text says* requires that students be able to trace the arc of a character's development over the course of a story, or accurately follow the chain of ideas and events that occur in an informational text **(standard 3)**. Doing so requires the reader to consolidate a number of sources of information, including words and phrases that signal a chronology or progression, and to accurately visualize the events as they transpire. All of this can tax working memory, especially when it comes to dense informational text. For example, a passage in a biology textbook is going to provide a detailed description of how neurons in the brain communicate with other cells at the synapse. Consider this paragraph from *The Brain: Our Nervous System,* a text used in a fifth grade science class:

> Because nerves don't touch one another, a message has to leap across a tiny gap called a synapse. A synapse is about a millionth of an inch wide and is a kind of living switch. When an electrical impulse reaches the knobby ends of the axon, it triggers the release of a chemical. This instantly jumps across the synapse to dendrites on the next nerve cell. The chemical causes the dendrites to trigger an electrical signal. The message continues through the cell body to the end of the axon, where it is passed from one neuron to many others along an almost endless number of pathways. Synapses always pass signals in the same direction; they cannot work in reverse. (Simon, 1997, p. 10)

The text-dependent questions posed by the teacher were intended to slow the reader down in order to correctly sequence this phenomenon. Her questions about the sequence of the events encouraged students to parse dense texts into manageable parts in order to understand them. For example, she asked the following questions:

- *Let's start by looking at that first sentence again. How does the signal move?*

- *The author compares the synapse to a switch. What would that mean it can do?*

- *Now let's trace the sequence of events in the messaging process. How does it begin?*

- *What is needed in order for the message to move from one neuron to another?*

- *If you're having trouble following the path, reread the fifth and sixth sentences.*

These literal-level questions, coupled with her prompts that assisted students in locating information, or reminded them to cite and name the evidence, built foundational knowledge about what was contained in the passage. The few extra minutes spent attending to the details of this pivotal paragraph set up the next portion of the passage, which is devoted to a discussion of what occurs neurologically when a person touches a hot surface. Later in the chapter, we will focus on questions about *what the text says* and how these questions can be used with complex texts in other elementary classrooms.

Language Standards

Language encompasses both speaking and writing, and the discussions that result from text-dependent questions have the power to build the language skills of students across both domains. As writing researcher James Britton remarked, "Writing floats on a sea of talk" (1983, p. 11).

Language **standard 1** focuses on students' command of standard English. In the primary grades, students are expected to use the conventions of language, such as marking plurals and applying verb tenses, and to move from simple to compound sentences. This is further delineated in grades 3–5 in terms of more complex grammatical structures, such as noun–verb agreements. Conventions are reinforced through consistent use of prompts during discussion, as students incorporate appropriate conventions into their speech.

Language **standard 3** focuses on how different language is used in different contexts, and is not described until grade 2, with attention to differentiating between informal and formal language. This is the beginning of an understanding of the language registers we use. Classroom discourse is usually *consultative*, meaning that discussion is at an academic level about concepts and phenomena that remain in the abstract. Events from the past are discussed in history, while physical, chemical, and biological phenomena are central in the sciences and universal themes permeate literature. Experience discussing abstract concepts and ideas is vital for students, who have a wealth of personal experiences, but who must learn to discuss abstract concepts and ideas in school. As well, discussion of nearly any text written in standard English provides students with the opportunity to replicate the syntax used by the author. The text-based discussions lead to the use of similar language structures in their written work.

Language **standard 6** concerns itself with the acquisition of academic language through reading and discussion. This includes descriptive language, words that signal relationships (e.g., *because*), and words that signal temporal and spatial relationships. The emphasis, over time, is on using language for communicating with precision and clarity. A list of the language standards that focus on *what the text says* is shown in Figure 2.2.

Speaking and Listening Standards

Without question, text-based discussions are at the core of the speaking and listening standards. **Standard 1** is all about participation in small- and large-group discussions. Importantly, text-dependent questions can be posed to the entire class, but explored more fully in small groups, before returning

Figure 2.2 Language Standards That Focus on *What the Text Says*

Kindergarten	Grade 1	Grade 2	Grade 3	Grade 4	Grade 5
1 Demonstrate command of the conventions of standard English grammar and usage when writing or speaking.	Demonstrate command of the conventions of standard English grammar and usage when writing or speaking.	Demonstrate command of the conventions of standard English grammar and usage when writing or speaking.	Demonstrate command of the conventions of standard English grammar and usage when writing or speaking.	Demonstrate command of the conventions of standard English grammar and usage when writing or speaking.	Demonstrate command of the conventions of standard English grammar and usage when writing or speaking.
a. Print many upper- and lowercase letters.	a. Print all upper- and lowercase letters.	a. Use collective nouns (e.g., *group*).	a. Explain the function of nouns, pronouns, verbs, adjectives, and adverbs in general and their functions in particular sentences.	a. Use relative pronouns (*who, whose, whom, which, that*) and relative adverbs (*where, when, why*).	a. Explain the function of conjunctions, prepositions, and interjections in general and their function in particular sentences.
b. Use frequently occurring nouns and verbs.	b. Use common, proper, and possessive nouns.	b. Form and use frequently occurring irregular plural nouns (e.g., *feet, children, teeth, mice, fish*).	b. Form and use regular and irregular plural nouns.	b. Form and use the progressive (e.g., *I was walking; I am walking; I will be walking*) verb tenses.	b. Form and use the perfect (e.g., *I had walked; I have walked; I will have walked*) verb tenses.
c. Form regular plural nouns orally by adding /s/ or /es/ (e.g., *dog, dogs; wish, wishes*).	c. Use singular and plural nouns with matching verbs in basic sentences (e.g., *He hops; We hop*).	c. Use reflexive pronouns (e.g., *myself, ourselves*).	c. Use abstract nouns (e.g., *childhood*).	c. Use modal auxiliaries (e.g., *can, may, must*) to convey various conditions.	c. Use verb tense to convey various times, sequences, states, and conditions.
d. Understand and use question words (interrogatives) (e.g., *who, what, where, when, why, how*).	d. Use personal, possessive, and indefinite pronouns (e.g., *I, me, my; they, them, their; anyone, everything*).	d. Form and use the past tense of frequently occurring irregular verbs (e.g., *sat, hid, told*).	d. Form and use regular and irregular verbs.	d. Order adjectives within sentences according to conventional patterns (e.g., *a small red bag* rather than *a red small bag*).	d. Recognize and correct inappropriate shifts in verb tense.
e. Use the most frequently occurring prepositions (e.g., *to, from, in, out, on, off, for, of, by, with*)	e. Use verbs to convey a sense of past, present, and future (e.g., *Yesterday I walked home; Today I walk home; Tomorrow I will walk home*).	e. Use adjectives and adverbs, and choose between them depending on what is to be modified.	e. Form and use the simple (e.g., *I walked; I walk; I will walk*) verb tenses.		
			f. Ensure subject-verb and pronoun-antecedent agreement.		

(Continued)

Figure 2.2 (Continued)

	Kindergarten	Grade 1	Grade 2	Grade 3	Grade 4	Grade 5
	f. Produce and expand complete sentences in shared language activities.	f. Use frequently occurring adjectives. g. Use frequently occurring conjunctions (e.g., and, but, or, so, because). h. Use determiners (e.g., articles, demonstratives). i. Use frequently occurring prepositions (e.g., during, beyond, toward). j. Produce and expand complete simple and compound declarative, interrogative, imperative, and exclamatory sentences in response to prompts.	f. Produce, expand, and rearrange complete simple and compound sentences (e.g., The boy watched the movie; The little boy watched the movie; The action movie was watched by the little boy).	g. Form and use comparative and superlative adjectives and adverbs, and choose between them depending on what is to be modified. h. Use coordinating and subordinating conjunctions. i. Produce simple, compound, and complex sentences.	e. Form and use prepositional phrases. f. Produce complete sentences, recognizing and correcting inappropriate fragments and run-ons. g. Correctly use frequently confused words (e.g., to, too, two; there, their).	e. Use correlative conjunctions (e.g., either/or, neither/nor).
3	(Begins in grade 2)	(Begins in grade 2)	Use knowledge of language and its conventions when writing, speaking, reading, or listening. a. Compare formal and informal uses of English.	Use knowledge of language and its conventions when writing, speaking, reading, or listening. a. Choose words and phrases for effect.	Use knowledge of language and its conventions when writing, speaking, reading, or listening. a. Choose words and phrases to convey ideas precisely.	Use knowledge of language and its conventions when writing, speaking, reading, or listening. a. Expand, combine, and reduce sentences

Kindergarten	Grade 1	Grade 2	Grade 3	Grade 4	Grade 5
			b. Recognize and observe differences between the conventions of spoken and written standard English.	b. Choose punctuation for effect. c. Differentiate between contexts that call for formal English (e.g., presenting ideas) and situations where informal discourse is appropriate (e.g., small-group discussion).	for meaning, reader/listener interest, and style. b. Compare and contrast the varieties of English (e.g., dialects, registers) used in stories, dramas, or poems.
6 Use words and phrases acquired through conversations, reading and being read to, and responding to texts.	Use words and phrases acquired through conversations, reading and being read to, and responding to texts, including using frequently occurring conjunctions to signal simple relationships (e.g., because).	Use words and phrases acquired through conversations, reading and being read to, and responding to texts, including using adjectives and adverbs to describe (e.g., When other kids are happy that makes me happy).	Acquire and use accurately grade-appropriate conversational, general academic, and domain specific words and phrases, including those that signal spatial and temporal relationships (e.g., After dinner that night we went looking for them).	Acquire and use accurately grade-appropriate general academic and domain-specific words and phrases, including those that signal precise actions, emotions, or states of being (e.g., quizzed, whined, stammered) and that are basic to a particular topic (e.g., wildlife, conservation, and endangered when discussing animal preservation).	Acquire and use accurately grade-appropriate general academic and domain-specific words and phrases, including those that signal contrast, addition, and other logical relationships (e.g., however, although, nevertheless, similarly, moreover, in addition).

Figure 2.3 Speaking and Listening Standards That Focus on *What the Text Says*

	Kindergarten	Grade 1	Grade 2	Grade 3	Grade 4	Grade 5
1	Participate in collaborative conversations with diverse partners about *kindergarten topics and texts* with peers and adults in small and larger groups. a. Follow agreed-upon rules for discussions (e.g., listening to others and taking turns speaking about the topics and texts under discussion). b. Continue a conversation through multiple exchanges.	Participate in collaborative conversations with diverse partners about *grade 1 topics and texts* with peers and adults in small and larger groups. a. Follow agreed-upon rules for discussions (e.g., listening to others with care, speaking one at a time about the topics and texts under discussion). b. Build on others' talk in conversations by responding to the comments of others through multiple exchanges. c. Ask questions to clear up any confusion about the topics and texts under discussion.	Participate in collaborative conversations with diverse partners about *grade 2 topics and texts* with peers and adults in small and larger groups. a. Follow agreed-upon rules for discussions (e.g., gaining the floor in respectful ways, listening to others with care, speaking one at a time about the topics and texts under discussion). b. Build on others' talk in conversations by linking their comments to the remarks of others. c. Ask for clarification and further explanation as needed about the topics and texts under discussion.	Engage effectively in a range of collaborative discussions (one-on-one, in groups, and teacher-led) with diverse partners on *grade 3 topics and texts*, building on others' ideas and expressing their own clearly. a. Come to discussions prepared, having read or studied required material; explicitly draw on that preparation and other information known about the topic to explore ideas under discussion. b. Follow agreed-upon rules for discussions (e.g., gaining the floor in respectful ways, listening to others with care, speaking one at a time about the topics and texts under discussion).	Engage effectively in a range of collaborative discussions (one-on-one, in groups, and teacher-led) with diverse partners on *grade 4 topics and texts*, building on others' ideas and expressing their own clearly. a. Come to discussions prepared, having read or studied required material; explicitly draw on that preparation and other information known about the topic to explore ideas under discussion. b. Follow agreed-upon rules for discussions and carry out assigned roles. c. Pose and respond to specific questions to clarify or follow up on information, and make comments that contribute	Engage effectively in a range of collaborative discussions (one-on-one, in groups, and teacher-led) with diverse partners on *grade 5 topics and texts*, building on others' ideas and expressing their own clearly. a. Come to discussions prepared, having read or studied required material; explicitly draw on that preparation and other information known about the topic to explore ideas under discussion. b. Follow agreed-upon rules for discussions and carry out assigned roles. c. Pose and respond to specific questions by making comments that contribute to the discussion and elaborate on the remarks of others.

	Kindergarten	Grade 1	Grade 2	Grade 3	Grade 4	Grade 5
				c. Ask questions to check understanding of information presented, stay on topic, and link their comments to the remarks of others. d. Explain their own ideas and understanding in light of the discussion.	to the discussion and link to the remarks of others. d. Review the key ideas expressed and explain their own ideas and understanding in light of the discussion.	d. Review the key ideas expressed and draw conclusions in light of information and knowledge gained from the discussions.
4	Describe familiar people, places, things, and events with prompting and support, provide additional detail.	Describe people, places, things, and events with relevant details, expressing ideas and feelings clearly.	Tell a story or recount an experience with appropriate facts and relevant, descriptive details, speaking audibly in coherent sentences.	Report on a topic or text, tell a story, or recount an experience with appropriate facts and relevant, descriptive details, speaking clearly at an understandable pace.	Report on a topic or text, tell a story, or recount an experience in an organized manner, using appropriate facts and relevant, descriptive details to support main ideas or themes; speak clearly at an understandable pace.	Report on a topic or text or present an opinion, sequencing ideas logically and using appropriate facts and relevant, descriptive details to support main ideas or themes; speak clearly at an understandable pace.
6	Speak audibly and express thoughts, feelings, and ideas clearly.	Produce complete sentences when appropriate to task and situation.	Produce complete sentences when appropriate to task and situation in order to provide requested detail or clarification.	Speak in complete sentences when appropriate to task and situation in order to provide requested detail or clarification.	Differentiate between contexts that call for formal English (e.g., presenting ideas) and situations where informal discourse is appropriate (e.g., small-group discussion); use formal English when appropriate to task and situation.	Adapt speech to a variety of contexts and tasks, using formal English when appropriate to task and situation.

once again to whole class debriefing. In fact, this is an excellent way to ensure that more students have an opportunity to participate. In these small group discussions, students are required to

- Refer to evidence from texts (1a)

- Pose and respond to questions (1c, begins in first grade)

- Consider the differing perspectives of multiple speakers (1d, begins in third grade)

Standard 4 addresses the presentation of information and evidence. This is not exclusively about formal presentation; it includes the extemporaneous speech of discussion. As students participate in discussion driven by text-dependent questions, they hone their ability to present ideas such that they are understood by others. The standards begin by calling for students to simply identify a sentence or short passage so that others can locate it. They then extend to address students' ability to recount a story or incident, and in the intermediate grades ask students to use relevant facts in an organized way to make themselves understood. **Standard 6** refers back to language **standards 1** and **3** (discussed in the previous section), especially in the way it emphasizes the importance of students' ability to speak in complete sentences and apply language registers appropriate to a given situation. Figure 2.3 contains a list of the speaking and listening standards that relate to *what the text says*.

Text-based discussions provide an initial starting point for exploring a reading in depth. Questions about the general understanding of the text, and the key details that frame it, invite students into the reading and allow those who are less sure to gain a firmer footing.

Using Text-Dependent Questions About *What the Text Says*

Helping students figure out *what the text says* requires attention to two main clusters of content:

- General understanding

- Key details

As we have noted, this is a good place from which to start when students encounter complex texts. Importantly, if students demonstrate their understanding of *what the text says* early on during a close reading, the teacher should leave this phase and move to the next one.

Questions About General Understanding

The first questions students consider when reading a new text are those that help them locate the literal level of meaning in the text, especially as it applies to plot and sequence. Understanding these elements then assists children as they accurately identify the main topic or main idea of the piece. Students must learn to identify the main idea, whether or not it is clearly and directly stated. For students in grades 4–5, a theme may not immediately make itself known. Questions that focus on the general understanding—the gist—are the place to begin.

> The first questions students consider when reading a new text are those that help them locate the literal level of meaning in the text, especially as it applies to plot and sequence.

These initial questions guide students to explore the information contained within the text. But teachers are also keeping one eye on the core message, which students may not get to until much later in the discussion. And that's OK. It's tempting to step in too early and tell them, "This text is really about the persistence and partnership of two explorers who faced challenges but were able to overcome obstacles in order to achieve." We get excited and we want them to get excited, too. But in their initial readings of a passage from *View From the Summit*, a memoir by Sir Edmund Hillary (2000), students probably won't identify the source of Hillary's discomfort as he describes receiving a British knighthood while Sherpa Tenzing Norgay did not. The teacher may understand the tension, but students may not. The goal is to not simply tell students this then, but to lay the groundwork so that students will be able to reach this understanding themselves as they delve deeper into the meaning of the text. To help them accomplish this, some of our general understanding questions steer them in this direction. For example,

> *How many times in this passage does Hillary describe Norgay's actions as they advanced toward the summit?*

And as they look back into the text, the teacher can remind students to list these actions, perhaps even cataloging them for later reference. As they go deeper, students will begin to understand the injustice of placing one man's achievement in front of another's. Although the two had agreed that they reached the peak of Everest together, media reports of the time profiled Hillary as the explorer and Norgay as the carrier of the supplies. "But we were not leader and led," Norgay wrote. "We were partners" (Norgay & Ullman, 1955, p. 46).

There will be time to get to *what the text means*, and this process begins by understanding what the text *says*.

Questions for General Understanding in Kindergarten and First Grade

The students in Steve Bradley's kindergarten class had just about finished listening to the second chapter of the text *Winnie-the-Pooh* (Milne, 1926), when Chase said, "That's really funny. He got stuck in the hole!" Already accustomed to reading and discussing texts closely, the students began talking about the main idea of the text. As Kiara noted, "I don't know what the main idea is. But the rabbit is funny."

Mr. Bradley asked them to begin their conversations with a discussion about the story arc. *"Let's start our discussion retelling what we know happens in the text. Try to retell the story in your own words. Start with the beginning, and try to recount it in order."*

As they did so, Mr. Bradley walked around the room listening to his students. As he considered the discussion in each partnership, he noted that they had a fairly strong understanding of the text in terms of the sequence of events that the author used to tell the story.

Students begin their conversations with a discussion about the story arc.

Had this not been the case, he would have reread the entire text, or a portion of the text, so that his students could deepen their discussion.

Satisfied that they understood the flow of events, Mr. Bradley interrupted the groups and asked, *"So what's the lesson here? You all understand the flow of ideas, but think about the lesson."*

As the students discussed this question, Mr. Bradley circulated around the room. Some partners were not quite where he wanted them to be; others were getting close to the understanding he was looking for. Then Michael raised his hand. Mr. Bradley asked if he needed something, and Michael said no, that he thought he had the answer. Mr. Bradley asked the other groups to listen in while Michael shared his thinking.

Michael started, saying, "So, in the beginning, Winnie-the-Pooh goes to Rabbit's house. And then he gets stuck in the hole because he ate too much. You can't eat everything or else you'll get stuck. That's the lesson. That's true. It could happen."

"But it's not a true story, right?" Brittney added. "You could get stuck if you ate too much but not the part about Pooh talking, right?"

Mr. Bradley responded, "Interesting. *So, if this is fiction like Brittney said, what is it that we should already know?* Maybe that's a better question for us to talk about. Go ahead and discuss that with your partners."

As Mr. Bradley listened to several students, he was pleased to hear their discussions about what they should understand. The discussions focused on the fact that they expected that there would be characters and that those characters would talk to each other. They also said that the story wasn't true, but that, in the story, there could be a lesson that was true.

> There will be time to get to *what the text means*, and this process begins by understanding what the text *says*.

Questions for General Understanding in Second and Third Grades

The students in Sonia Perez's second and third grade combination class looked up at her in mild shock. They had just finished an initial reading of the text, *Hey, Little Ant* (Hoose & Hoose, 1998). Ms. Perez reminded her students to annotate on the text itself, a one-page listing of all of the words from the text found in the back of the book. As she walked around the room, she noted that her students were not circling any words or phrases, an indicator that they understood the words the author used.

She invited them to talk with a partner, saying, *"Let's start with a conversation about the information in the text. What happens? In your own words, take turns and explain the events in this text."*

"So, it starts off kinda babyish," Sabrina said. "The boy is talking to an ant about squishing him."

"And the ant talks back, saying why he should not die," Marlon added.

"But then it doesn't end," David said. "We don't know what happened, and the author makes us think about it."

To build on their initial understanding, Ms. Perez posed several questions designed to shift their attention to the source: *Who is the author? What type of text is it? Why was it written?* Quick discussion of these points led students to some new conclusions. They noted that the authors were father and daughter and that they wrote the text as a song. As Ms. Perez listened to the students' discussions, she reminded them to update their annotations so that they could use their notes later. To ensure that they did this, *Ms. Perez asked her students to summarize the message in three or fewer sentences.* She read over their shoulders as they did so, noting that her students understood that the kid was a bully. She also noted that none of her students recognized the peer pressure aspect of the text.

Questions for General Understanding in Fourth and Fifth Grades

As part of their investigation about the Revolutionary War, the students in Ashley Washington's fifth grade class read an excerpt from the speech containing the phrase, "Give me liberty or give me death," delivered by Patrick Henry on March 23, 1775. They understood a lot of the factual information related to the formation of the American colonies as well as general information about the Revolutionary War, but Ms. Washington wanted her students to gain an understanding of the perspective of a person who lived during this time. As she often said, "History is a story well told."

She provided her students with several paragraphs from the text so that they could annotate directly on it. As she distributed the text, she asked them to *"try to identify Henry's main message."* This question about general understanding provided them with a concrete task and focus as they did their initial reading of the text.

A quick look at the students' annotations revealed their ability to underline key ideas as well as to identify words and phrases that were confusing. In this case, students grasped the message of the text from their initial reading and discussions.

As is common when students work with primary source documents, they began their reading focused on the main message of the text. Ms. Washington instructed, *"As you read this speech for the first time, focus on the message. Ask yourself, what is he trying to tell the people? Remember that we always read considering the source and the context."*

Listening in to one group, Ms. Washington noted that they focused on the reasons that Patrick Henry wanted to go to war.

"I think that the big idea here is that Americans have to come together to solve the problems of their time," Mariah said. "He's really asking for help from everyone."

"I agree, because he says the 'the millions of people, armed in the holy cause of liberty' are really powerful. He really thinks that they will win, but that they have to start fighting right away," Marcus added.

"And he says if they don't do this, they'll end up being slaves to Britain," Kadra said. "In the first part, he says that they have been making chains for a long time, and then later he says that if they try to go back they will be beat, because the chains are already there, ready."

"So, we know that the war really did happen, but he says that it is inevitable, like it was going to happen no matter what," Mariah said. "How do you think he knew that?'"

Having visited a few groups, Ms. Washington decided to call the class back together. She signaled for them to finish their conversations and said, *"I'm going to ask for one person from each group to summarize the general ideas in the text in one sentence. Reach agreement about that and then I'll call on folks to respond."* When Kadra was called on, her group had agreed on the following: "Patrick Henry had thought that they should go to war with Great Britain because the British were already starting a war against them."

Questions About Key Details

Each text contains details that are essential to understanding the broader meaning of the text. We don't just mean interesting details, but rather those that are linked to the main idea or central theme. Students sometimes have difficulty in sorting out the difference between key details and merely interesting ones. Text-dependent questions about the key details guide students toward an understanding of the differences between the two. The text type drives the type of key details readers are seeking. In a narrative text type, the key details are linked to the story grammars: What are the plot

Students sometimes have difficulty in sorting out the difference between key details and merely interesting ones.

lines, characters, setting, and such? In an informational piece, the key details are attached to the organizational patterns, such as problem–solution, cause and effect, compare–contrast, and so on. These narrative and expository text structures are not always apparent to students and are explored more completely when the conversation moves forward to examine how a text *works*. Therefore, the questions about key details ask students about the "five Ws"—*who, what, when, where,* and *why*. Related key detail questions ask students the "how" questions—*how much? How many?*

Questions About Key Details in Kindergarten and First Grade

As he usually does, Mr. Bradley had a number of key details questions ready for his students as they read and discussed Chapter 2 from *Winnie-the-Pooh* (Milne, 1926). He knew that he might not need to use all of the questions he had prepared, but having them at the ready guided his interactions with students, especially when they were not able to figure out the answers. He started with a where-and-when question: *"Where does this story take place?"* The students talked with each other and quickly identified the answer.

Then he focused their attention on the characters, saying, *"Let's talk about the people in this story. Who are the main characters? But maybe even more importantly, what role does each character play in the story?"*

Some students turned their attention to Rabbit, while others focused on Pooh, and still others focused on Christopher Robin.

"Rabbit doesn't want Pooh to come in because he eats everything," said Hunter. "He pretends not to be home."

"Christopher Robin is a friend," Stephanie added. "He reads a book to Winnie-the-Pooh until Pooh gets skinny enough to get out."

"Yeah, he's helpful," Jasmine said.

Hearing this, Mr. Bradley paused the conversations and asked Jasmine to share her comment with the rest of the class. After she spoke, Mr. Bradley asked the class, *"So, what do we think about this character trait? Do you agree or disagree with Jasmine?"*

Samantha, turning to her partner Brian, said, "I agree, because he stayed for a whole week to help Winnie." Brian responded, "Me, too.

The text type drives the type of key details readers are seeking.

I agree, because he didn't get mad when Winnie-the-Pooh got stuck. He just helped."

As their conversations about the characters in the text slowed down, Mr. Bradley asked his students the final key detail question: *Why does the text say that Rabbit doesn't answer Pooh at first? Many of you talked about Pooh eating all of the food, but what does the text say?* The students look puzzled and talk with each other about Pooh eating all of the food. Mr. Bradley then reread aloud a section of the text in which Rabbit says, "You know how it is. One can't have *anybody* coming into one's house. One has to be *careful*" (p. 26). Mr. Bradley asks the question again, *Why does the text say that Rabbit doesn't answer Pooh at first?* This time the students had it, and immediately talked about letting strangers in the house. Mr. Bradley, concluding this part of the lesson, said, "This helps us practice our listening skills. Some times we have to go back and make sure we know what the author really said. We can think about other reasons as well, but we want to be sure to understand *what the text says*. Sometimes it's hard to remember, so we'll read that chapter again tomorrow, just like we did with Chapter 1, so we really understand it."

Questions About Key Details in Second and Third Grades

The text-dependent questions posed to the class shifted to focus on key details. Ms. Perez asked students to read *Hey, Little Ant* (Hoose & Hoose, 1998) again, this time with an eye toward key details that would yield insights into the characters of the kid and the ant. The class had been studying about characters and how an author portrays them in different ways. As the class finished reading, Ms. Perez introduced two language charts to help students analyze the two main characters (see Figure 2.4). In the past, Ms. Perez would have distributed this for students to use independently. But that would have reduced the opportunity to coconstruct knowledge and would have resulted in some students doing well but too many others still struggling. *"Let's start by looking for some of those key details about the characters,"* she said. *"Keep in mind we're looking for evidence, too. Let's start by talking about the physical descriptions the authors gave us for the kid and the ant."* Following their discussion about the obvious physical characteristics, students selected other aspects to discuss. Several students were intrigued by the dialogue.

Figure 2.4 Character Analysis Language Chart for Key Details

Title and Author of Text: _____

Character's Name: _____

Things We Know About the Character	Examples	What This Says About the Character
Physical Description		
Dialogue		
Thoughts		
Reactions of Others		
Actions		

Available for download from **www.corwin.com/textdependentquestions**

"They talk back to each other with their own ideas," Javier said.

"And that is how we know what they think," Patrice added. "It's like they listen to the other one and then think of what to say next."

"Yeah, I agree," Sarah said. "But then I was thinking about the other kids. I think they want him to do it, so they are giving him pressure."

"Oh, that's it," Javier said. "It's pressure from the other kids. But what about the ant? What about other ants?"

"We really don't know," Patrice said. "He is strong and digs the nest and feeds the babies, but it doesn't say anything about the reactions of the other ants."

The students hadn't yet settled on the meaning of the ending, but Ms. Perez knew they were moving in the right direction. This initial general understanding and the key detail questions weren't the end of the learning, but the students were building a foundation of shared knowledge. As she steered the discussion toward a closer examination of *how the text worked*—namely in terms of vocabulary and text structure—she was confident they would close in on the meaning.

Questions About Key Details in Fourth and Fifth Grades

The students in Ms. Washington's class had a reasonably strong general understanding of the text, so she decided to ask them two questions to further check their understanding.

"You all really got the big message from the text, so let's see how the details help us understand it a bit more," she said. "Let's talk about two things. First, where in the text does Henry say that others might disagree with him? And second, describe the actions that Henry believes the colonists have already taken to avoid fighting with the British.

"Let's go back into the text and look for this information. It may not be right there, on one specific line, but these are important details that will help us understand the overall point the author is trying to make."

The students returned to the text and began highlighting their findings. Kevin began the conversation for his group.

"Henry says that others will probably disagree in the second sentence. He says, 'But different men often see the same subject in different lights.' That means that people might not agree on the same subject; he just says it more fancy."

"He also says, 'I hope it will not be thought disrespectful to those gentlemen if, entertaining as I do opinions of a character very opposite to theirs,'" said Tamara. "That means he doesn't mean to be rude, but that he doesn't agree with some of the other people. Maybe they're in the room or maybe they talked before him, because he says, 'The very worthy gentlemen who have just addressed the House.'"

As they discussed their responses to the text, Ms. Washington visited with various groups asking them clarifying questions, such as, *"What does he mean that he has one lamp to guide his feet?"* and *"Why does he say 'This is no time for ceremony'?"* Based on her interactions with various groups, she was confident that her students understood what the text said at the literal level. She knew that they had skipped some of the more complex vocabulary and planned to address those terms as she moved to Phase 2—*how the text works*. Ms. Washington knew that her students were developing their understanding of the text while also developing habits that would serve them well as they transitioned to middle school.

As they discuss their responses to the text, the teacher visits with various groups asking clarifying questions.

QUESTION YOURSELF

This chapter has focused on the role of literal questions as a starting place for close reading. We have made the case that general understanding and key detail questions can be used later in the lesson to understand more nuanced information in a text. We have focused on the differences between general understanding and the key details that are important in gaining that understanding.

Now, we invite you to practice yourself. Figure 2.5 shows Robert Louis Stevenson's poem "My Shadow." You can use this to apply what you have learned. First, take a minute or two and read the poem. Then turn your attention to think about the questions that you can develop to encourage students to analyze *what the text says*. Remember that this phase is focused on general understanding and key details. Determine what is it that students should know about this text before inviting them to explore the ways in which the text works, which will be the focus of our next chapter.

Before you begin, you might like to skim the italicized questions in the teachers' lessons, above. If you'd like to check yourself, the questions that Ms. Thayre developed can be found in this book's Appendix III and at www.corwin.com/textdependentquestions. Then, apply this technique to develop questions for a short piece that you will use with your own students.

Figure 2.5 "My Shadow" by Robert Louis Stevenson

I have a little shadow that goes in and out with me,
And what can be the use of him is more than I can see.
He is very, very like me from the heels up to the head;
And I see him jump before me, when I jump into my bed.

The funniest thing about him is the way he likes to grow—
Not at all like proper children, which is always very slow;
For he sometimes shoots up taller like an india-rubber ball,
And he sometimes gets so little that there's none of him at all.

He hasn't got a notion of how children ought to play,
And can only make a fool of me in every sort of way.
He stays so close beside me, he's a coward you can see;
I'd think shame to stick to nursie as that shadow sticks to me!

One morning, very early, before the sun was up,
I rose and found the shining dew on every buttercup;
But my lazy little shadow, like an arrant sleepy-head,
Had stayed at home behind me and was fast asleep in bed.

Available for download from **www.corwin.com/textdependentquestions**

Videos

To read a QR code, you must have a smartphone or tablet with a camera. We recommend that you download a QR code reader app that is made specifically for your phone or tablet brand.

Videos can also be accessed at
www.corwin.com/textdependentquestions

Video 2.1 Students in Lisa Forehand's kindergarten class discuss their opinions based on their first reading of *The Day the Crayons Quit.*

Video 2.2 Students in Alex Cabrera's second grade class discuss the concept of supply and demand based on an article they read about cow farmers.

Video 2.3 Shawna Codrington asks her second grade students to review the setting and characters in *Lon Po Po*, the Chinese version of *Little Red Riding Hood.*

Video 2.4 Melissa Noble's fourth grade class analyzes the sequence of events using the annotations they made during their close read of "Why Wisdom Is Found Everywhere."

3

HOW DOES THE TEXT **WORK**?

A bridge is a powerful symbol for most of us. It connotes movement from one place to another. It offers reliable passage across an otherwise difficult divide. It marks a path for travel. When we encounter a bridge, we cross it. The urge to do so is deeply rooted in our nature. Metaphorically, bridges represent transitions, paths, or connections. And this is exactly what questions focused on *how the text works* do for students.

Attention to how a text works can provide students with a cognitive bridge as they travel from the literal meaning (*what the text says*) to the inferential (*what the text means*). The journey from literal to inferential understanding requires analysis, and the divide between the two can be rocky. In fact, more than a few students can lose their way without a clear path and a good guide. But text-dependent questions help by casting a light on the vocabulary, structure, and craft used by a writer to convey a message.

To borrow a term introduced by Adler and Van Doren (1940/1972), questions about *how the text works* allow us to "x-ray the book" (p. 75). These questions prompt children to look beyond what is at the surface in order to more closely examine the internal workings of the text. If determining *what the text says* is analogous to inspection, then figuring out *how the text works* is similar to investigation. Consider what a crime scene investigator does. After inspecting the scene and determining that the incident cannot be easily explained, she begins to collect evidence. She uses these samples to reconstruct what has occurred. She knows what to look for (the footage from a security camera, a set of footprints near a broken window) and keeps her eyes open for more subtle trace evidence that she can find using special techniques, such as dusting for fingerprints. These practices help her to reconstruct what might have happened leading up to the crime. She's not ready to formulate conclusions, but this investigation is an essential step in her process toward understanding what happened.

> Questions about *how the text works* allow us to "x-ray the book" (Adler & Van Doren, 1940/1972, p. 75). These questions prompt children to look beyond what is at the surface.

An Invitation to Read Closely: *Structural*-Level Questions

Analytic reading requires in part that the reader take the text apart and then reassemble it. By probing the parts, readers can begin to understand the whole. While it is true that the whole text is more than the sum of its parts, the practice of unearthing components that are likely to be important is critical to understanding the text as a whole. But simply making piles of parts is insufficient. That would be deconstruction, without reconstruction. The analysis must also include how the parts fit into the whole. The first is a pile of bricks, while the second is a complete house (Adler & Van Doren, 1940/1972).

Discussion about vocabulary, text structure, and author's craft serves as the bridge to understanding the text as a whole. The text-dependent questions for these discussions bear some functional similarities to *adjunct questions*, which are written questions that are interspersed throughout a text in order to draw the reader's attention to an element of the passage. Several studies have demonstrated positive effects on the comprehension of older readers who are provided adjunct questions (e.g., Chi & Bassock, 1989; Peverly & Wood, 2001). Their usefulness lies in their ability to shift a reader's attention to an element of the text the reader may have overlooked, especially in the case of students termed *low structure builders* (Callender & McDaniel, 2007). *Structure building* is a construct proposed by Gernsbacher (1991) which describes comprehension as a process that

> involves building a coherent structure out of the presented information. This process involves laying a foundation with the initial information that is read and mapping the new information onto the existing structure. When information is encountered that is not conceptually related to the existing structure . . . the reader shifts and builds a new substructure. This is done repeatedly throughout the text resulting in a mental representation, or structure of the text. (Callender & McDaniel, 2007, p. 340)

Discussion about vocabulary, text structure, and author's craft serves as the bridge to understanding the text as a whole.

Poor structure builders have a difficult time assembling these substructures into a coherent whole. How can we help? To aid reading comprehension, intersperse adjunct questions *and* add the power of discussion. Nystrand's (2006) analysis of 150 years of research on the effects of discussion on reading comprehension confirmed what many teachers already realize: "The relative ineffectiveness of recitation and other monologic practices in teaching reading comprehension, compared to discussion and instructional conversation, [means that] meaning is realized only in the process of active, responsive understanding" (p. 400). In other words, naming the piles (recitation) does little to enable structure building. Discussion in small and large groups aids students in assembling the substructures in order to understand the piece.

To aid reading comprehension, add the power of discussion.

Why Students Need This Type of Questioning

Elements that underpin a text include its *expository or literary structures and features,* and *vocabulary words and phrases.* These components are intentionally selected by skilled writers to convey experience, inform, or persuade. Think of these as the bones of the text, as they hold up the ideas and concepts presented. These elements organize a text and properly channel the flow of information such that the reader can follow its internal logic.

But it is this framework that often eludes young readers and writers. These elements may seem invisible to them, because when the elements are skillfully utilized, they are a backdrop to the action. Take signal words for example. Most elementary students are in the process of learning that signal words let readers know the organizing text structure, in the same way that flags mark out the course for a downhill skier. Sets of signal words such as *first, then, next,* and *last* are used to organize sequenced text; the presence of an *if . . . then* pairing means it is a problem–solution text structure. But some of these more obvious signal words give way in upper grades to texts that use more subtle forms. In their places, words like *simultaneously* and *previously* signal not only a chronology, but also that the writer has altered the time order. A problem may be described as a *dilemma*, and its solution may not be discussed until many paragraphs or even chapters later.

Text-dependent questions focus students on the organizational structures and word choices that organize the text. But they also make more apparent what it is the writer is *doing*, something collectively referred to as *author's craft*. Skilled writers select organizational structures and make word choices to serve their purposes, in the same way that a builder selects materials to construct a house. Who will live there? What weather conditions must the house be able to endure? Even skilled readers have difficulty employing the elements of good writing, in part because they may not be consciously attending to them. Questions that shift students' attention to the inner workings of a text can have the cumulative effect of raising their consciousness as writers. Hansen (2001) notes that when students read as writers, they make decisions about how they themselves will enact these same craft moves.

> Most elementary students are in the process of learning that signal words let readers know the organizing text structure, in the same way that flags mark out the course for a downhill skier.

How Examining *How the Text Works* Addresses the STANDARDS

Reading Standards

The cluster of reading standards entitled "craft and structure" lie at the heart of this second cognitive path. **Standard 4** focuses on words and phrases, while **standard 5** addresses text features in literature and informational texts and in expository text structures. **Standard 6** examines how authors establish a point of view. The intent of **standard 4** in the primary grades is to introduce children to words and phrases in literary and informational texts, especially as these words and phrases relate to word choice and effect. Students in grades 2–5 are introduced to literary terms such as *alliteration, simile,* and *metaphor*. The intent of **standard 5** is to draw back a bit further from words and phrases to examine how text features work in both print and digital environments. For example, students are expected to develop an understanding of hyperlinks and search tools in grade 3. In terms of literature, organizational features such as *chapter* and *stanza* are named. **Standard 6** concerns itself with how point of view is established within and across characters or people. Children in the primary grades identify point of view in a story and learn about the different contributions from the illustrator and author. By fifth grade, students are examining multiple accounts of the same event. See Figure 3.1 for the grade-specific standards for grades K–5.

The kindergarten students in Cindy Abrams's class had been in school for just a month, and they were developing their knowledge of how books work. She had established a routine with her students about how they examine a book, beginning with the parts. She had read *The Important Book* (Brown, 1949) to them, they had discussed the general meaning and key details, and now they were returning to the structures.

"Let's look at the details about the book to learn more about it. Think about how you find out who the author and the illustrator are."

Although several children wanted to call out the answer, she reminded them to "talk with your elbow partner about where you find the information."

Ms. Abrams listened in on several conversations and then posed the question again to the group, this time requesting that one student show the class. Tyana used the pointer to show where the information is located on the front cover of the book.

"Now let's look at the back cover," said the teacher. *"There's more information here about the author, named Margaret Wise Brown, and the illustrator, Leonard Weisgard. I'll read this to you so we can learn more about these two people who made this beautiful book for us."*

Later, Ms. Abrams said, "Although most of them are at the earliest stages of emergent literacy, they are already understanding how books are structured. I want to get them in the habit of looking all around the book, not just inside, to find out interesting things."

Figure 3.1   ELA Reading Standards That Focus on *How the Text Works*

Standard (Grade)	Literary	Informational
4 (K)	Ask and answer questions about unknown words in a text.	With prompting and support, ask and answer questions about unknown words in a text.
4 (1)	Identify words and phrases in stories or poems that suggest feelings or appeal to the senses.	Ask and answer questions to help determine or clarify the meaning of words and phrases in a text.
4 (2)	Describe how words and phrases (e.g., regular beats, alliteration, rhymes, repeated lines) supply rhythm and meaning in a story, poem, or song.	Determine the meaning of words and phrases in a text relevant to a *grade 2 topic or subject area*.
4 (3)	Determine the meaning of words and phrases as they are used in a text, distinguishing literal from nonliteral language.	Determine the meaning of general academic and domain-specific words and phrases in a text relevant to a *grade 3 topic or subject area*.
4 (4)	Determine the meaning of words and phrases as they are used in a text, including those that allude to significant characters found in mythology (e.g., Herculean).	Determine the meaning of general academic and domain-specific words or phrases in a text relevant to a *grade 4 topic or subject area*.
4 (5)	Determine the meaning of words and phrases as they are used in a text, including figurative language such as metaphors and similes.	Determine the meaning of general academic and domain-specific words and phrases in a text relevant to a *grade 5 topic or subject area*.
5 (K)	Recognize common types of texts (e.g., storybooks, poems).	Identify the front cover, back cover, and title page of a book.
5 (1)	Explain major differences between books that tell stories and books that give information, drawing on a wide reading of a range of text types.	Know and use various text features (e.g., headings, tables of contents, glossaries, electronic menus, icons) to locate key facts or information in a text.
5 (2)	Describe the overall structure of a story, including describing how the beginning introduces the story and the ending concludes the action.	Know and use various text features (e.g., captions, bold print, subheadings, glossaries, indexes, electronic menus, icons) to locate key facts or information in a text efficiently.
5 (3)	Refer to parts of stories, dramas, and poems when writing or speaking about a text, using terms such as chapter, scene, and stanza; describe how each successive part builds on earlier sections.	Use text features and search tools (e.g., key words, sidebars, hyperlinks) to locate information relevant to a given topic efficiently.
5 (4)	Explain major differences between poems, drama, and prose, and refer to the structural elements of poems (e.g., verse, rhythm, meter) and drama (e.g., casts of characters, settings, descriptions, dialogue, stage directions) when writing or speaking about a text.	Describe the overall structure (e.g., chronology, comparison, cause/effect, problem/solution) of events, ideas, concepts, or information in a text or part of a text.

Standard (Grade)	Literary	Informational
5 (5)	Explain how a series of chapters, scenes, or stanzas fits together to provide the overall structure of a particular story, drama, or poem.	Compare and contrast the overall structure (e.g., chronology, comparison, cause/effect, problem/solution) of events, ideas, concepts, or information in two or more texts.
6 (K)	With prompting and support, name the author and illustrator of a story and define the role of each in telling the story.	Name the author and illustrator of a text and define the role of each in presenting the ideas or information in a text.
6 (1)	Identify who is telling the story at various points in a text.	Distinguish between information provided by pictures or other illustrations and information provided by the words in a text.
6 (2)	Acknowledge differences in the points of view of characters, including by speaking in a different voice for each character when reading dialogue aloud.	Identify the main purpose of a text, including what the author wants to answer, explain, or describe.
6 (3)	Distinguish their own point of view from that of the narrator or those of the characters.	Distinguish their own point of view from that of the author of a text.
6 (4)	Compare and contrast the point of view from which different stories are narrated, including the difference between first- and third-person narrations.	Compare and contrast a firsthand and secondhand account of the same event or topic; describe the differences in focus and the information provided.
6 (5)	Describe how a narrator's or speaker's point of view influences how events are described.	Analyze multiple accounts of the same event or topic, noting important similarities and differences in the point of view they represent.
10 (K)	Actively engage in group reading activities with purpose and understanding.	
10 (1)	With prompting and support, read prose and poetry of appropriate complexity for grade 1.	With prompting and support, read informational texts appropriately complex for grade 1.
10 (2)	By the end of the year, read and comprehend literature, including stories and poetry, in the grades 2–3 text complexity band proficiently, with scaffolding as needed at the high end of the range.	By the end of year, read and comprehend informational texts, including history/social studies, science, and technical texts, in the grades 2–3 text complexity band proficiently, with scaffolding as needed at the high end of the range.
10 (3)	By the end of the year, read and comprehend literature, including stories, dramas, and poetry, at the high end of the grades 2–3 text complexity band independently and proficiently.	By the end of the year, read and comprehend informational texts, including history/social studies, science, and technical texts, at the high end of the grades 2–3 text complexity band independently and proficiently.
10 (4)	By the end of the year, read and comprehend literature, including stories, dramas, and poetry, in the grades 4–5 text complexity band proficiently, with scaffolding as needed at the high end of the range.	By the end of year, read and comprehend informational texts, including history/social studies, science, and technical texts, in the grades 4–5 text complexity band proficiently, with scaffolding as needed at the high end of the range.

Language Standards

While reading spotlights one mode of literacy, language encompasses all: reading, writing, speaking, and listening. The language standards that hone in on discovering *how a text works* flow directly from those discussed in the previous section on reading. The elementary version of **standard 3** describes the importance of listening, reading, and writing for clarity and consistency. (Keep in mind that this standard doesn't apply until second grade). **Standards 4** and **6** are clustered around vocabulary acquisition and use. Collectively, these standards require students to use structural and contextual analysis to resolve unknown words and phrases, turning to resources as needed in pursuit of new vocabulary. **Standard 5** closely parallels the reading standards described in the previous section, especially as it relates to word relationships and figurative language. A table of the targeted language standards for grades K–5 can be found in Figure 3.2.

The third grade students in Elena Arshun's class had been reading and discussing poems that reflected distinct settings, with a special focus on contrasting those written about rural and urban environments. In addition, Ms. Arshun was creating opportunities for her students to explore how writers use words in imaginative ways. She and her students had read the poem "Concrete Mixers" by Patricia Hubbell (in Prelutsky, 1983) and had focused on the key detail of the poet's comparison of a concrete mixer to an elephant.

She had defined the word *mahout* for them already, so they knew this meant a person who rides an elephant, thereby assisting them in understanding the comparison to the driver of a large concrete mixer. "*Let's look at this more closely,*" said the teacher. "*What are other words and phrases the poet uses to compare the two?*"

Initially, the students focused on the explicitly stated examples, such as *move, bellow,* and *spray* like elephants. "*But what does bellow mean?*" she asked. The students were stumped, but the teacher didn't immediately define it for them. "*I'm going to add that to the words we might need to investigate,*" she said as she wrote it on the board.

Her students soon turned their collective attention to the poet's comparisons to the physical appearance, especially in describing both the color and the tough outer surface of the elephant and the concrete mixer.

Garrett compared their behavior. "They both spray something . . ."

" . . . like a elephant sprays water out of his nose, and the concrete mixer sprays all the wet concrete," Leann finished his thought.

Now the teacher returned to the subject of the unknown word, *bellow.* "*I want to summarize your comparisons,*" she said. "*You talked about their movement, that they're both slow and heavy. And you said they were gray and had a tough outside surface. Now let's think about another characteristic we haven't discussed. How do you know there's an elephant nearby, or a concrete mixer nearby, even before you see it? Talk with each other.*"

Figure 3.2 Language Standards That Focus on *How the Text Works*

	Kindergarten	Grade 1	Grade 2	Grade 3	Grade 4	Grade 5
3	(Begins in grade 2)	(Begins in grade 2)	Use knowledge of language and its conventions when writing, speaking, reading, or listening. a. Compare formal and informal uses of English.	Use knowledge of language and its conventions when writing, speaking, reading, or listening. a. Choose words and phrases for effect. b. Recognize and observe differences between the conventions of spoken and written standard English.	Use knowledge of language and its conventions when writing, speaking, reading, or listening. a. Choose words and phrases to convey ideas precisely. b. Choose punctuation for effect. c. Differentiate between contexts that call for formal English (e.g., presenting ideas) and situations where informal discourse is appropriate (e.g., small-group discussion).	Use knowledge of language and its conventions when writing, speaking, reading, or listening. a. Expand, combine, and reduce sentences for meaning, reader/listener interest, and style. b. Compare and contrast the varieties of English (e.g., dialects, registers) used in stories, dramas, or poems.
4	Determine or clarify the meaning of unknown and multiple-meaning words and phrases based on *kindergarten reading and content.* a. Identify new meanings for familiar words and apply them accurately	Determine or clarify the meaning of unknown and multiple-meaning words and phrases based on *grade 1 reading and content,* choosing flexibly from an array of strategies. a. Use sentence-level context as a clue to the meaning	Determine or clarify the meaning of unknown and multiple-meaning words and phrases based on *grade 2 reading and content,* choosing flexibly from an array of strategies. a. Use sentence-level context as a clue to the meaning of a word or phrase.	Determine or clarify the meaning of unknown and multiple-meaning words and phrases based on *grade 3 reading and content,* choosing flexibly from a range of strategies. a. Use sentence-level context as a clue to the meaning	Determine or clarify the meaning of unknown and multiple-meaning words and phrases based on *grade 4 reading and content,* choosing flexibly from a range of strategies. a. Use context (e.g., definitions, examples, or restatements in text) as a clue to	Determine or clarify the meaning of unknown and multiple-meaning words and phrases based on *grade 5 reading and content,* choosing flexibly from a range of strategies. a. Use context (e.g., cause/effect relationships and comparisons

(Continued)

Figure 3.2 (Continued)

Kindergarten	Grade 1	Grade 2	Grade 3	Grade 4	Grade 5
(e.g., knowing *duck* is a bird and learning the verb to *duck*). b. Use the most frequently occurring inflections and affixes (e.g., -ed, -s, re-, un-, pre-, -ful, -less) as a clue to the meaning of an unknown word.	of a word or phrase. b. Use frequently occurring affixes as a clue to the meaning of a word. c. Identify frequently occurring root words (e.g., *look*) and their inflectional forms (e.g., *looks, looked, looking*).	b. Determine the meaning of the new word formed when a known prefix is added to a known word (e.g., *happy/unhappy, tell/retell*). c. Use a known root word as a clue to the meaning of an unknown word with the same root (e.g., *addition, additional*). d. Use knowledge of the meaning of individual words to predict the meaning of compound words (e.g., *birdhouse, lighthouse, housefly; bookshelf, notebook, bookmark*). e. Use glossaries and beginning dictionaries, both print and digital, to determine or clarify the meaning of words and phrases.	of a word or phrase. b. Determine the meaning of the new word formed when a known affix is added to a known word (e.g., *agreeable/ disagreeable, comfortable/ uncomfortable, care/careless, heat/preheat*). c. Use a known root word as a clue to the meaning of an unknown word with the same root (e.g., *company, companion*). d. Use glossaries or beginning dictionaries, both print and digital, to determine or clarify the precise meaning of key words and phrases.	the meaning of a word or phrase. b. Use common, grade-appropriate Greek and Latin affixes and roots as clues to the meaning of a word (e.g., *telegraph, photograph, autograph*). c. Consult reference materials (e.g., dictionaries, glossaries, thesauruses), both print and digital, to find the pronunciation and determine or clarify the precise meaning of key words and phrases.	in text) as a clue to the meaning of a word or phrase. b. Use common, grade-appropriate Greek and Latin affixes and roots as clues to the meaning of a word (e.g., *photograph, photosynthesis*). c. Consult reference materials (e.g., dictionaries, glossaries, thesauruses), both print and digital, to find the pronunciation and determine or clarify the precise meaning of key words and phrases.

Kindergarten	Grade 1	Grade 2	Grade 3	Grade 4	Grade 5
5 With guidance and support from adults, explore word relationships and nuances in word meanings.	With guidance and support from adults, demonstrate understanding of word relationships and nuances in word meanings.	Demonstrate understanding of word relationships and nuances in word meanings.	Demonstrate understanding of word relationships and nuances in word meanings.	Demonstrate understanding of figurative language, word relationships, and nuances in word meanings.	Demonstrate understanding of figurative language, word relationships, and nuances in word meanings.
a. Sort common objects into categories (e.g., shapes, foods) to gain a sense of the concepts the categories represent.	a. Sort words into categories (e.g., colors, clothing) to gain a sense of the concepts the categories represent.	a. Identify real-life connections between words and their use (e.g., describe foods that are *spicy or juicy*).	a. Distinguish the literal and nonliteral meanings of words and phrases in context (e.g., *take steps*).	a. Explain the meaning of simple similes and metaphors (e.g., *as pretty as a picture*) in context.	a. Interpret figurative language, including similes and metaphors, in context.
b. Demonstrate understanding of frequently occurring verbs and adjectives by relating them to their opposites (antonyms).	b. Define words by category and by one or more key attributes (e.g., *a duck is a bird that swims; a tiger is a large cat with stripes*).	b. Distinguish shades of meaning among closely related verbs (e.g., *toss, throw, hurl*) and closely related adjectives (e.g., *thin, slender, skinny, scrawny*).	b. Identify real-life connections between words and their use (e.g., describe people who are *friendly or helpful*).	b. Recognize and explain the meaning of common idioms, adages, and proverbs.	b. Recognize and explain the meaning of common idioms, adages, and proverbs.
c. Identify real-life connections between words and their use (e.g., note places at school that are *colorful*).	c. Identify real-life connections between words and their use (e.g., note places at home that are *cozy*).		c. Distinguish shades of meaning among related words that describe states of mind or degrees of certainty (e.g., *knew, believed, suspected, heard, wondered*).	c. Demonstrate understanding of words by relating them to their opposites (antonyms) and to words with similar but not identical meanings (synonyms).	c. Use the relationship between particular words (e.g., synonyms, antonyms, homographs) to better understand each of the words.

(Continued)

Figure 3.2 (Continued)

	Kindergarten	Grade 1	Grade 2	Grade 3	Grade 4	Grade 5
	d. Distinguish shades of meaning among verbs describing the same general action (e.g., *walk, march, strut, prance*) by acting out the meanings.	d. Distinguish shades of meaning among verbs differing in manner (e.g., *look, peek, glance, stare, glare, scowl*) and adjectives differing in intensity (e.g., *large, gigantic*) by defining or choosing them or by acting out the meanings.				
6	Use words and phrases acquired through conversations, reading and being read to, and responding to texts.	Use words and phrases acquired through conversations, reading and being read to, and responding to texts, including using frequently occurring conjunctions to signal simple relationships (e.g., *because*).	Use words and phrases acquired through conversations, reading and being read to, and responding to texts, including using adjectives and adverbs to describe (e.g., *When other kids are happy that makes me happy*).	Acquire and use accurately grade-appropriate conversational, general academic, and domain specific words and phrases, including those that signal spatial and temporal relationships (e.g., *After dinner that night we went looking for them*).	Acquire and use accurately grade-appropriate general academic and domain-specific words and phrases, including those that signal precise actions, emotions, or states of being (e.g., *quizzed, whined, stammered*) and that are basic to a particular topic (e.g., *wildlife, conservation, and endangered* when discussing animal preservation).	Acquire and use accurately grade-appropriate general academic and domain-specific words and phrases, including those that signal contrast, addition, and other logical relationships (e.g., *however, although, nevertheless, similarly, moreover, in addition*).

It doesn't take them long to narrow it down to two possibilities—smell or sound. "*So now let's go back to the poem. Perhaps we can figure out which one it might be,*" said Ms. Arshun. "*Bellow like an elephant,*" she read. "*Does a concrete mixer sound like an elephant or smell like an elephant?*"

Now the students are beginning to understand the word—it's a sound. "It's a big sound, like arggarggargg . . ." laughed Oliver, trying to imitate the truck.

Now Ms. Arshun was ready to use the dictionary. "*It says it's a deep roar, usually in anger or in pain,*" she read to them. "*Now you can add that to the words you use in your writing. Maybe someone will use* bellow *in a story they write this week?*" suggested the teacher.

Speaking and Listening Standards

The standards profiled previously in Chapter 2 remain the same when discussing how a text works. As with other aspects of a close reading process, it is discussion that elevates this from rudimentary independent work to true discourse. Unlike simple question-and-answer exchanges that rarely evolve past recitation and recall, text-based discussion provides learners with the opportunity to hone their listening skills in small and large groups, and to participate as coconstructors of knowledge. Figure 3.3 contains a list of the speaking and listening standards addressed in text-based discussions of *how the text works*.

Figure 3.3　Speaking and Listening Standards That Focus on *How the Text Works*

	Kindergarten	Grade 1	Grade 2	Grade 3	Grade 4	Grade 5
1	Participate in collaborative conversations with diverse partners about *kindergarten topics and texts* with peers and adults in small and larger groups. a. Follow agreed-upon rules for discussions (e.g., listening to others and taking turns speaking about the topics and texts under discussion). b. Continue a conversation through multiple exchanges.	Participate in collaborative conversations with diverse partners about *grade 1 topics and texts* with peers and adults in small and larger groups. a. Follow agreed-upon rules for discussions (e.g., listening to others with care, speaking one at a time about the topics and texts under discussion). b. Build on others' talk in conversations by responding to the comments of others through multiple exchanges. c. Ask questions to clear up any confusion	Participate in collaborative conversations with diverse partners about *grade 2 topics and texts* with peers and adults in small and larger groups. a. Follow agreed-upon rules for discussions (e.g., gaining the floor in respectful ways, listening to others with care, speaking one at a time about the topics and texts under discussion). b. Build on others' talk in conversations by linking their comments to the remarks of others. c. Ask for clarification and further explanation	Engage effectively in a range of collaborative discussions (one-on-one, in groups, and teacher-led) with diverse partners on *grade 3 topics and texts*, building on others' ideas and expressing their own clearly. a. Come to discussions prepared, having read or studied required material; explicitly draw on that preparation and other information known about the topic to explore ideas under discussion. b. Follow agreed-upon rules for discussions (e.g., gaining the floor in respectful ways, listening to others with care, speaking one at a time about the topics and texts under discussion).	Engage effectively in a range of collaborative discussions (one-on-one, in groups, and teacher-led) with diverse partners on *grade 4 topics and texts*, building on others' ideas and expressing their own clearly. a. Come to discussions prepared, having read or studied required material; explicitly draw on that preparation and other information known about the topic to explore ideas under discussion. b. Follow agreed-upon rules for discussions and carry out assigned roles. c. Pose and respond to specific questions to clarify or follow up on	Engage effectively in a range of collaborative discussions (one-on-one, in groups, and teacher-led) with diverse partners on *grade 5 topics and texts*, building on others' ideas and expressing their own clearly. a. Come to discussions prepared, having read or studied required material; explicitly draw on that preparation and other information known about the topic to explore ideas under discussion. b. Follow agreed-upon rules for discussions and carry out assigned roles. c. Pose and respond to specific questions by making comments that contribute to the discussion and elaborate on the remarks of others.

	Kindergarten	Grade 1	Grade 2	Grade 3	Grade 4	Grade 5
		about the topics and texts under discussion.	as needed about the topics and texts under discussion.	c. Ask questions to check understanding of information presented, stay on topic, and link their comments to the remarks of others. d. Explain their own ideas and understanding in light of the discussion.	information, and make comments that contribute to the discussion and link to the remarks of others. d. Review the key ideas expressed and explain their own ideas and understanding in light of the discussion.	d. Review the key ideas expressed and draw conclusions in light of information and knowledge gained from the discussions.
4	Describe familiar people, places, things, and events and, with prompting and support, provide additional detail.	Describe people, places, things, and events with relevant details, expressing ideas and feelings clearly.	Tell a story or recount an experience with appropriate facts and relevant, descriptive details, speaking audibly in coherent sentences.	Report on a topic or text, tell a story, or recount an experience with appropriate facts and relevant, descriptive details, speaking clearly at an understandable pace.	Report on a topic or text, tell a story, or recount an experience in an organized manner, using appropriate facts and relevant, descriptive details to support main ideas or themes; speak clearly at an understandable pace.	Report on a topic or text or present an opinion, sequencing ideas logically and using appropriate facts and relevant, descriptive details to support main ideas or themes; speak clearly at an understandable pace.
6	Speak audibly and express thoughts, feelings, and ideas clearly.	Produce complete sentences when appropriate to task and situation.	Produce complete sentences when appropriate to task and situation in order to provide requested detail or clarification.	Speak in complete sentences when appropriate to task and situation in order to provide requested detail or clarification.	Differentiate between contexts that call for formal English (e.g., presenting ideas) and situations where informal discourse is appropriate (e.g., small-group discussion); use formal English when appropriate to task and situation.	Adapt speech to a variety of contexts and tasks, using formal English when appropriate to task and situation.

Viewed collectively, text-dependent questions about the vocabulary, text structure, and author's craft build a bridge for students to mentally traverse as they move from *what the text says* to *what the text means*. The critical thinking needed to make the leap to levels 3 and 4 in the Depth of Knowledge framework does not come easily. In fact, our experience has been that traditionally higher achieving readers may balk at some of these questions, because they are more accustomed to focusing on the literal-level meaning of the text. When teachers press for evidence from the text to questions that focus on *how the text works*, students must consider the structures that the author used to create the text, which in turn leads to deeper understanding of the text.

Using Text-Dependent Questions About *How the Text Works*

Helping students figure out *how the text works* requires attention to three main clusters of content:

- Vocabulary

- Text structures

- Author's craft

That's not to say that all texts are complex in these ways or that teachers have to ask questions in each of these areas. It is to say that teachers can analyze the texts for their internal workings, considering vocabulary, text structure, and author's craft, to determine the specific questions that they can ask to help students deepen their understanding of the text or to assess students' developing proficiency with the standards.

Questions About Vocabulary

One significant predictor of reading comprehension is vocabulary (Baumann, Kame'enui, & Ash, 2003). Simply said, if a reader knows the meaning of the words, the text is more likely to be understood. That doesn't mean that students should already know all of the words and phrases before they read a complex text. Students learn a lot of words and phrases from the reading that they do (White, Graves, & Slater, 1990). Mason, Stahl, Au, and Herman (2003) estimate that a student can learn about 2,250 new words per year while reading. Interestingly, these same researchers estimate that students can learn between 300 and 500 words through systematic instruction. As Adams (1990) noted,

> While affirming the value of classroom instruction in vocabulary, we must also recognize its limitations. By our best estimates, the growth in recognition vocabulary of the school age child typically exceeds 3,000 words per year, or more than eight per day. This order of growth cannot be ascribed to their classroom instruction, nor could it be attained through any feasible program of classroom instruction. (p. 172)

Close reading of complex texts is one of the activities in which students can learn a lot of words. Of course, wide independent reading is another activity in which students can learn a lot of words, and we would be remiss if we did not point out that teachers have to carefully select the words that they are going to directly teach, given that students don't learn a lot of words this way.

We are not suggesting that close reading become a time for vocabulary instruction. We are suggesting that there be time for direct and systematic vocabulary instruction but that it occurs outside of the close reading lesson. During close readings, the text-dependent questions that teachers ask allow students to practice and apply their word-solving skills. As noted in language **standard 4,** students should be able to "determine or clarify the meaning of unknown and multiple-meaning words and phrases by using context clues, analyzing meaningful word parts, and consulting general and specialized reference materials, as appropriate" (CCSSI, 2010a, p. 25). Solving for unknown words is one of the habits that students need to develop if they are going to be successful with reading closely.

During close readings, the text-dependent questions that teachers ask allow students to practice and apply their word-solving skills.

This starts with an identification of the terms that may trip up students. If there are words that cannot be easily solved, the teacher may simply provide students with a definition on the bottom of the page. For example, during their reading of *Casey at the Bat* (Thayer, 1888/2000), Amy Stringer provided her students with a margin note that included the definitions of *melancholy* and *doffed*. She decided that they weren't essential words for students to focus on, and she knew that the contextual and structural clues were not helpful. Providing students with access to the meaning of these words while they were reading and rereading the text allowed them to focus on the meaning of the text. There were plenty of other words and phrases that deserved her students' cognitive attention.

Later, on their third read of the poem, Ms. Stringer invited her students to use their iPads to find the meaning of several words and phrases, including *patrons, haughty grandeur,* and *charity*. As they used this resource, the meaning of the text became clearer. As Ms. Stringer said,

> By the time we get out the iPads to find the meanings of words, the students have a lot of knowledge from the text, and they're looking for definitions that make sense. It's really more inquiry based than me just telling them the meaning of the words, hoping that they'll remember them and be able to use the definitions. And, if I really think about it, it's what I do when I read. I have to figure out the meaning of the text, and sometimes that means I have to reread and figure out the words the author is using.

As we have noted, the text-dependent questions should focus on both words and phrases. Sometimes it's worth the time to focus on individual words. Other times, it's important to consider phrases. Confusion does not exist only at the word level, and the standards are specific in the attention to words and phrases, as well as to students' ability to "demonstrate understanding of figurative language, word relationships, and nuances in word meanings" (CCSSI, 2010a, p. 25). Just think how easy each word in the idiom "hit the books" is, but simply understanding each word will not result in students understanding that they should be studying. Knowledge of the vocabulary deepens the reader's understanding of the text, and not only through definition.

Knowledge of the vocabulary deepens the reader's understanding of the text, and not only through definition.

Questions About Vocabulary in Kindergarten and First Grade

Mr. Bradley's analysis of Chapter 2 of *Winnie-the-Pooh* (Milne, 1926) suggested that vocabulary would not be a significant barrier for his students. As he expected, they listened to the text with ease and were able to discuss their general understanding and the key details of the text.

Then he read the text aloud a second time. Mr. Bradley was interested in exploring a sentence from the text: "Then would you read a Sustaining Book, such as would help and comfort a Wedged Bear in Great Tightness?" (p. 30). So he asked his students to discuss what it meant.

"Let's take apart this sentence. And let's start with 'you.' Who is 'you'?"

As the students discussed this, Mr. Bradley noted that one of the groups thought *you* referred to Rabbit, but the others correctly identified Christopher Robin. Mr. Bradley asked one of the groups with the correct answer to explain the thinking behind their decision.

"I think it's Christopher Robin because of the sentence before where he says that we will read to you. Christopher Robin is talking," Hunter said.

Kiara raised her hand, offering, "But it *could* be Rabbit, because it says 'we,' but it probably is Christopher Robin because that's who is talking."

Mr. Bradley, satisfied that they understood the pronoun referent, followed up with the question, *"So what does it mean—'Wedged Bear in Great Tightness'? Those are pretty big words, so make sure that you use your context clues."*

As the students discussed their responses, Mr. Bradley joined the group that had the incorrect response to the first question. He interrupted their conversation and asked if the pronoun referent made sense to them, and what the phrase meant. The students in the group indicated that they did now understand it probably referred to Christopher Robin. When asked about the phrase, Chase said, "We think it's about being stuck, because he says tightness, but we don't really know all of those words."

Bringing the class back together, Mr. Bradley asked for volunteers to talk about the phrase *'Wedged Bear in Great Tightness.'*

Brittney was the first to volunteer. "My grandma says that a lot, like wedged in the cabinet and wedged in a parking spot. It's kind of like you got to get it fit in."

"Oh, so like he almost didn't fit?" Angela responded.

"Yeah," Brittney answered.

Mr. Bradley then asked the class if that made more sense to them. *"So can someone tell me what that phrase means?"*

This time Brian offered to answer. "It just means that he's stuck in the hole, right?"

"You got it," said Mr. Bradley. *"Any other phrases that are a bit confusing that you remember? We can talk about them, if you want."*

Questions About Vocabulary in Second and Third Grades

Sonia Perez's students returned to the picture book *Hey, Little Ant* (Hoose & Hoose, 1998) the following day, this time by seeing the pictures in the text projected using a document camera. Ms. Perez said to her students, *"You've already read the words that the author used. Today, we'll look more closely at the words and how the illustrator decided to show the ideas from the text. Before we do that, I want to clear up a few confusing words. When I looked over your annotations last night, I noticed that several of you circled* nest mates*. Let's take a closer look at that phrase and figure out what it means."*

Immediately, the students started talking.

"I don't really know what it means," Sabrina said, "but I didn't circle it, so I should now."

"I circled it but now I think that it's the other ants because of the picture we saw," Joseph commented.

"I think it's like a roommate, because they're all living together," Javier added.

"But why do they say *nest?*" Sabrina asked. "Do ants make a nest like birds?" Sabrina raised her hand to call Ms. Perez over and repeated her question, "Do ants make nests?"

"That's a great question," Ms. Perez responded. *"If you knew that answer, it would probably help you with the phrase, right? Why don't you Google that, and then let the rest of the class know."*

Sabrina and her group quickly opened iPads and searched for *ant nests*. They found millions of pages and illustrations. Sabrina raised her hand to get Ms. Perez's attention. "We found the answer. Wanna see?"

Mr. Perez asked for attention from the rest of the class. "Boys and girls, Sabrina and her group found some information that might help you in your discussions about this phrase. Sabrina, go ahead."

"So, we found out that ants live in nests, but not like bird nests. They don't build them out of sticks and stuff. They dig a nest. Nest mates are the other ants that live in the same colony."

Ms. Perez, thanking Sabrina and her group, turned to the class. *"That was the only phrase that several of you circled. But some of you have individual words that you circled. In your groups, can you check each other's papers to make sure that you understand all of the words?"*

Again, the students started discussing the vocabulary from their text.

As part of their interaction with the text, students circle words and phrases that are confusing to them.

Questions About Vocabulary in Fourth and Fifth Grades

The "Give Me Liberty or Give Me Death" speech has a lot of very difficult vocabulary words. Given that Ashley Washington's fifth grade students read this text well into the school year, their habits with annotation were already strong. As part of their interaction with the text, they circled words and phrases that were confusing to them. Ms. Washington had already told them that *sentiments* meant a person's beliefs or opinions; that *solace* was comfort, especially in times of stress; that *beseech* meant to ask someone urgently; and that *extenuate* was to make something less serious. She expected that her students would not immediately know the meaning of *accumulation*, *supplication*, *supinely*, and *delusive phantom*, but she was not worried about those terms, as they did not distract from her students' initial understanding of the text.

To check their understanding of the text through vocabulary, Ms. Washington asked her students, *"What does Patrick Henry beseech of his listeners?"*

The students talked about this and clearly understood what the word meant. For example, Tamara said, "He really wants them to start the fight, the war, with the British and to do it right away."

Ms. Washington then turned their attention to one of the complex phrases in the text, saying, *"There is an interesting phrase in this speech: 'so formidable an adversary.' We really haven't talked about what Patrick Henry means by this. What are you thinking? I know that many of you circled this, but now that you've explored this text more deeply, what are you thinking?"*

Jessie started the conversation for his group. "I think it's saying that they are strong, because he says that they, meaning the British, say that we, meaning the Americans, are weak."

"I agree with you, because it says in the next line, 'When shall we be stronger?' So they must be stronger," Paul added.

"But can we look it up?" Mariah asked. "I think it's more than that, but I'm not sure why. I agree that it means that they are stronger, but I kinda think *adversary* means *enemy*. Let's check."

Ms. Washington then asked students to review the words they had circled and to discuss them at their tables. *"Make sure that the people in your group all have the same knowledge about vocabulary. We've read this a few times now, so now let's make sure that the words are solid. If there is a word that no one in your group knows, please write it on a card, and I'll come by to collect the cards."*

The conversations among the groups of students continued as they negotiated the meaning of several words, with Kadra's group writing *supinely* on a card, because none of the members of their group understood that word. Ms. Washington knew that she would have to come back around to the vocabulary again on a subsequent reading to ensure that students were applying their knowledge of words and phrases to the text. But time was nearly up for the day, and she wanted to check their understanding, so she asked students to write a response to the following prompt on the back of their papers:

"What is the situation in colonies such that Patrick Henry is compelled to give this speech?"

Questions About Structure

The opening sections of this chapter contain a great deal of information about the importance of considering text structures in planning close reading lessons. During their elementary school years, students should become familiar with the basic story grammar of narrative texts (e.g., character, plot, setting, problem, actions, resolution) as well as common informational text structures, such as compare and contrast, problem and solution, cause and effect, sequence, and description. (See Figure 3.4 for a list of common expository text structures.) As texts become more complex, so do their structures. Narrative texts involve increasingly complex plots, with numerous characters as well as intricate dialogue and narrative elements. (Narrative elements are covered more thoroughly in the next section.) Increasingly complex informational texts use multiple text structures across paragraphs rather than solely focusing on a cause and effect, for example. In addition, these informational texts often differ based on the discipline in which they were developed. For example, science texts often rely on generalization and classification, whereas historical texts beg for corroboration and contextualization.

As texts become more complex, so do their structures.

Figure 3.4   Common Expository Text Structures

Text Structure	Definition
Compare–contrast	A text that describes the similarities and differences among two or more things, places, events, ideas, people, or other factors.
Problem–solution	A text that identifies an issue and how the issue is solved. Often the solution becomes another problem.
Cause–effect	A text that explains how or why something happened, in terms of both the root cause and the impact of that cause.
Chronological/sequence/temporal	This text presents information as a process or in order of time or sequence.
Descriptive	This text provides details that could be a list or outline.

Available for download from **www.corwin.com/textdependentquestions**

We will return to the classrooms that were introduced in Chapter 2 to observe the ways in which teachers deepened students' understanding by focusing on the structures of the texts. In some cases, the teacher moved to this phase during the same lesson, and in other cases the teacher reengaged students on a subsequent day, returning to the text.

Questions About Structure in Kindergarten and First Grade

Mr. Bradley's students understood that their text, *Winnie-the-Pooh* (Milne, 1926), was a fictional story. They had talked about the structure the author used, especially a chronological telling of the events. Mr. Bradley invited them to discuss how the reading experience was different when the author used dialogue versus when the narrator took over.

"We've read this twice now. *I'd like to start our next discussion about the difference between characters talking—we know that's called dialogue— versus when the narrator tells us something. Can you talk with each other about the differences and what you learn from each?*"

"I like it when the characters talk. It seems more real," Chase noted.

"The narrator tells you the story," Michael said.

"When the characters talk, you can learn about what they want or what they are thinking," Brandi said.

Satisfied that his students understood this important difference, Mr. Bradley asked his students, "*Can you remember parts of the story where the narrator is talking? And can you remember other parts of the story when it's dialogue between the characters? Turn to your conversation partner and see what you can each remember.*"

"Like in the beginning, when it starts, it's the narrator because, remember, he says he was doing his exercises," Kiara said.

"When Winnie-the-Pooh goes to Rabbit's house, the characters are talking, because Winnie says 'are you home,' and Rabbit says 'no.'" Angela added.

In another group Samantha and Brian talked about the times that Christopher Robin said "Silly old bear."

"The narrator wouldn't really say that. He could say 'he was a silly old bear,' but when he gets hisself stuck, that's when Christopher Robin says it, 'silly old bear,'" Samantha said.

Mr. Bradley is pleased to know that the instruction he has provided regarding narrators and characters has allowed his students to analyze the text accordingly. He also knows, and has evidence from each of his students, that they can differentiate fairly effectively between narrative and expository texts. Mr. Bradley also recognizes that his students need more work in developing their understanding of subtypes of texts, which he plans to address in the units that follow his close reading of *Winnie-the-Pooh*.

Questions About Structure in Second and Third Grades

Sonia Perez's combination class had been reading *Hey, Little Ant* and had discussed what the text says. Next, they were ready to investigate *how the text works*.

"Let's look at the structure of the text for a moment," offered Ms. Perez. *"You know that this started as a song. But what other structures are you noticing? Be sure to annotate them on your copies of the text."*

As her students reread, Ms. Perez observed where they were marking their papers, as she hoped they would recognize the stanzas and rhymes. After a few minutes, she invited her students to talk with one another.

"It's like a poem! It even has stanzas. They're separated," Marlon said.

"Yeah, wow, there's even spaces between every four lines," Sarah added. "I was thinking about a song because of the top part with the music. You're right."

Ms. Perez brought the class back together, saying, "Every group I visited was able to identify the major structure of the text. For groups that I wasn't able to visit, what did you notice?"

Sarah raised her hand and when called on said, "It's written in stanzas, right? There's a space after every four lines and they're numbered to 11."

Ms. Perez called on another student at random, "Joseph, what did you hear Sarah say, and do you agree?"

After Joseph responded correctly, Ms. Perez changed the direction of the conversation. "You're all becoming much more skilled at analyzing text structures. I hope you are recognizing that in yourselves. In fact, why don't you give yourselves a hand? [The students clap for a few seconds.] *I'm interested in your noticing other things about the structure. You said it was both a poem and song. Often, but not always, authors use internal structures so that readers and listeners know where the stanzas are. I'd like one member from each table to read the text aloud to the other members of the group. You can decide who you want to be your reader.*"

In their group, Patrice was asked to be the reader, and she read the text aloud to the other members of her group.

"It's a rhyme," Christine said excitedly when Patrice finished. "I guess that I kinda didn't pay attention to it. Every two lines rhyme. When you read it out loud, I heard it."

"Yeah, I missed that, too," David added. "I can see the words that rhyme. Some of the words have the same spelling at the end, and others don't."

"Oh, like *chips* and *lips* have the same ending, but *too* and *shoe* don't, but they sound like they could. Let's look at all of the lines," Patrice suggested.

"I think we should make a list of the pairs that have the same spelling and the ones that are different," Christine added. "I bet that's what Ms. Perez will tell us to do next anyway."

This group was right. As part of her close reading lesson, Ms. Perez provided students time to explore spelling patterns from the text they were reading. Different groups created different recording tools. Some used t-charts, while others used lists. Their format didn't much matter to Ms. Perez, who knew that her students were developing their abilities to analyze texts.

Questions About Structure in Fourth and Fifth Grades

Ms. Washington's students, as part of their discussion about what the text meant, discussed the fact that "Give Me Liberty or Give Me Death" was told in first person, and the text provided the perspective of Patrick Henry himself. So Ms. Washington knew that she did not need to ask her students about point of view or perspective. She wanted her students to read primary source documents as historians do, specifically engaging in the following practices (Wineburg, Martin, & Monte-Sano, 2011):

1. *Sourcing:* Analyzing the author's point of view, when and why a document was written, and the credibility of the source.

2. *Contextualization:* Considering the setting and identifying what else was happening historically or socially at that time.

3. *Corroboration:* Considering what other pieces of evidence say or analyzing another version of the same event.

She has been using this framework all year, so her students will develop habits about examining historical documents, artifacts, and visuals. With these goals in mind, Ms. Washington focused her students on more than the literal level of understanding when they first encountered the text. It is important for students to understand what the text says, but this is not sufficient to ensure that they read like historians. The second (and third) phase of close reading allows students to develop their historical and scientific thinking skills.

> The second (and third) phase of close reading allows students to develop their historical and scientific thinking skills.

Questions about the structure of the text can help students understand the *source* of the text and consider some aspects of the *context* of the text. In Ms. Washington's classroom, in which students are reading the Patrick Henry speech, she asked her students, *"From your read of the text, and your analysis of the structure, what can you say about the source, Patrick Henry? I'd like you to start with reviewing the text and making some additional margin notes or annotations about this, and then talk with your groups."*

After they had reviewed the text again, Noah began. "I think he's credible, because he was talking to some government thing, like a group. [Noah checks the text.] Yeah, the House, because he has 'addressed the House,' so that means the House of Representatives. There's a big conflict going on between the people in the colonies and the British. The speech is said so that people can understand his point of view. And he's making sure they know that he understands what the problems are."

"I think it's pretty obvious why he gave this speech—he even says 'I shall speak,'" Kevin added. "But I disagree with Noah, because they were colonies and didn't have their freedom from England yet, and they didn't have the constitution, so I'm not sure what the House means, but I don't think it's the House of Representatives."

Ms. Washington paused the groups. *"We'll learn more about what they meant by House when we read the textbook. We'll also look at some other sources from the time as we move through this unit. I appreciate the comments about the historical time, our corroboration, because that helps us understand the text even better."* She recognized that her students were thinking about the structures of the text and were developing the same habits that historians use to understand the meaning behind texts.

Questions about the author's craft have the potential for impacting the writing students do.

Questions About Author's Craft

Craft is that which separates good writing from bad writing and effective arguments from ineffective ones. We all know writers who exhibit exceptional craft as well as writers who are more amateurish. Developing students' understanding of author's craft helps them understand texts more deeply. For example, if the author uses symbolism that is missed by the reader, part of the message, or the impact of that message, is lost. But perhaps even more important, questions about the author's craft have the potential for impacting the writing students do. When they understand the impact that various craft moves have on the reader, novice writers begin to incorporate those moves in their own compositions.

There is a wide range of tools at an individual author's disposal. These include these literary and poetic devices (which can overlap):

- Genres and the specific features of these genres

- The ways in which specific words and phrases contribute to mood and tone

- The role of the narrator

- Sentence length and rhythm

- Text features, such as charts, figures, and diagrams

Some of these are presented in Figure 3.5. For example, the way an author uses a narrator can contribute to understanding or confusion. Edgar Allen Poe was famous for using an unreliable narrator in his short stories, adding a great deal of confusion. Zusak (2005) used Death as the narrator in *The Book Thief* and provided the narrator with omniscient understanding of the historical events as well as the human condition. In *Out of the Dust* (Hesse, 1997), the narrator is 13-year-old Billie Jo, and the story is told entirely in first person, using open verse. In the middle of the book *Rose Blanche* (Gallaz & Innocenti, 1985), a story about a German girl living during the Holocaust, the author switches from first person to third person, which forces the reader to analyze the events in the text differently. These are conscious choices that authors make, choices that readers must contend with.

Some genres are more familiar or consumable than others. As any reader of *The Day the Crayons Quit* (Daywalt, 2013) can attest, an epistolary (story told through letters) is complex. Sometimes authors blur the lines between genres, as is the case in the Newbury Award book *Flora and Ulysses* (DiCamillo, 2013), which mixes narrative text in chapter book form with comic strips and illustrations. Similarly, readers have to take note when an author explodes the moment to slow down the action through the use of extensive details. Sometimes authors use sentence structure and length to engender physical response.

Informational text often contains supporting photographs, captions, and diagrams. Imagine reading almost anything from a *National Geographic* magazine issue without the stunning visuals and detailed maps. These text features are a part of the author's craft as sure as the written text, as they are integral to the presentation of information. Readers can be challenged to integrate information when it is presented across multiple elements, such as illustrations, end papers, and such.

As we have noted, attention to author's craft facilitates students' understanding of the text as well as their ability to compose

Figure 3.5   Sample of Author's Craft Components

Literary Devices	Allegory
	Allusion
	Cliffhanger
	Flashback
	Foreshadowing
	Imagery
	Irony and satire
	Point of view
	Time lapse
	Tone and mood
Unique Structures	Writing in diary or journal style
	Quotes or famous sayings
	Using dates or unique ways to identify chapters
	Enumerating an argument
	Prologue and epilogue/coda
Poetic Devices	Alliteration
	Hyperbole
	Metaphor
	Onomatopoeia
	Personification
	Repetition
	Simile
	Symbolism
Text Features	Charts
	Diagrams
	Figures
	Illustrations
	Boldface or italicized words
	Font
Narration	First person, second person, third person
	Limited, omniscient, unreliable

Available for download from **www.corwin.com/textdependentquestions**

increasingly sophisticated prose, narrations, and informative texts. Text-dependent questions about such elements can shift students' focus to the moves a writer makes, and over time spill into the students' own writing.

Questions About Author's Craft in Kindergarten and First Grade

Mr. Bradley focused on the author's use of humor as his students explored *Winnie-the-Pooh* (Milne, 1926). He started with this question:

"When does our author use humor? We've been talking about different ways that writers make a connection with their readers. And humor is one of the ways that we talked about. We've even practiced telling jokes to other people, like our parents. So, let's review our text and look for humor. Do you remember where it was?"

Zoe started the conversation. "I think that he uses humor when Winnie-the-Pooh gets out of the hole. They all fall on top and make a big pile."

"Yeah, that was funny," Mr. Bradley said. *"Can you picture it in your mind?* Winnie pops out really fast and all of the people pulling fall on top of each other. *Humor helps us remember things. What else?"*

"And when Rabbit says somebody ate too much and it wasn't me!" Brian added. "Because the way he says it made me laugh."

Angela jumped into the conversation. "And then, when they say he has to stay for a whole week, Christopher Robin says 'silly old bear' and then you can stay in there but you can't get out."

The conversation continued with discussion about the ways in which the author used humor and how the humor helped students remember different parts of the text. As part of this discussion, Mr. Bradley showed his students the illustrations that accompanied the text. The students especially liked the illustration of the towels hanging from Winnie-the-Pooh's feet inside Rabbit's house.

As Hunter noted, "I remember that part! Rabbit said he could put towels on his feet because he was stuck. But how could his feet hold still?"

"We've talked about characterization used by the author to give us some insight," said Ms. Perez. "We know a lot about the two characters. When I was listening to your groups, I heard some people say that the point of view changes. *Do you agree or disagree that the point of view changes?"*

For the next few minutes, the class discussed the point of view used by the author. As Javier noted, "I don't agree, because both characters say 'I' and so that means the character's talking. Maybe some people thought that it changed because there are two different characters that both say 'I,' but that doesn't mean they're not telling the story."

"I agree with you," Christine added, "because it says 'I,' but it is just different characters talking for each page."

"Now let's go a bit further. Let's review the illustrations to see how the author uses size to tell part of the story," said Ms. Perez.

In small groups, the students discussed each of the illustrations, while Ms. Perez prompted their thinking. *"What are you seeing in the first image about size?"*

"Well, the ant is tiny, and the boy is normal," Cassandra said.

"And on the next page, the ant is still small but bigger than the page before," Kasim added.

"And the ant is in the shadow of the boy," Sarah commented.

As they progressed through the text, they continued to focus on the size differences. When they came to the point in the text where the ant asked the boy to decide what is right and what is wrong, their conversation changed.

"I missed that before," Kasim said. "Now the ant is giant and the boy is really small. It's like it means the ant is the boss. It says, what would you do if 'you were me and I were you,' but, I don't know, it's like it's more important."

"It really shows that you have to think what you want that other person to do," Sarah responded.

"Yeah, because it's more real," Cassandra added. "Like the ant could really squish you. It makes you think about it, because it is more real, like it could happen."

After allowing the table discussions to progress for several minutes over several pages of text, Ms. Perez said, "Welcome back to all of you. I was listening in on your conversations and I heard lots of comments about size and how the author uses the illustrations to add emphasis. Before we leave this, *let's talk about how the characters in this text change. They change over the course of the text, so pick a couple of lines to talk about with your group. How does each character change, and what evidence do you have?"*

The students' conversation continued, and they noted that the boy started off as aggressive and mean, but he was pleading when the ant was talking. Other words students used described the boy as a bully at the beginning of the text but as a character who by the end wasn't so sure of himself. The students in Ms. Perez's class were used to discussing how the characters change in a text, as she regularly talked with them about what she notices while she reads.

Questions About Author's Craft in Fourth and Fifth Grades

Ms. Washington's students demonstrated fairly sophisticated analysis of the text structure of the "Give Me Liberty or Give Me Death" speech and had explored the role of the narrator and first person perspectives. In other words, they had engaged in the type of thinking that Wineburg, Martin, and Monte-Sano (2011) suggest about sourcing the material. They understood the perspective of the author. They also understood the context in which the piece was written, as they had been studying this period of history for several weeks and had made connections, early on during their discussion about what the text says, between the speech and what was happening in the colonies at the time. What they hadn't discussed was why the text was written. Ms. Washington asked her students, *"How does the speaker's point of view influence the content of the speech?"*

"It explains a lot," Jessie said. "He was the guy who was against the Stamp Act from Britain. He was also part of the Boston Tea Party. So, he had really strong ideas about what should happen. He liked to fight for his ideas."

"Yeah, so we don't know what the average person in the colonies thought or what people in Britain thought," Eileen responded. "We know that he was trying to convince people to go to war, because he was very against the British."

"And that's probably why he has so many details," Mariah added. "The details make it more believable, because people could check on the details to see if they're true. And the details would maybe tell people that it was facts, that he wasn't biased."

"I totally get it now," Jose commented. "This is his point of view, so he gives this speech to try to convince people that he is right and that the colonies should go to war."

In response, Ms. Washington said, "Interesting conversations. I'm hearing a lot of talk about the author, who he was, and how his point of view shows up in this speech. I'd also like to talk about the devices that he uses. *We've been studying literary and poetic devices for quite some time. Let's look back to our analysis tools. Remember that we can focus on devices such as repetition and restatement as well as on metaphor and images. What do you all see?*"

Wendy was the first to speak in her group. "Repetition. He says the same thing over again. I really didn't notice that the first time, but then I underlined those times, like when he says 'let it come' or 'we must fight.' I think it makes you pay more attention."

"Yeah, I agree," Jose added. "I can picture that in my mind, like the second time he says it different. Maybe slower or louder or something so that people really get it."

In another group Eileen commented, "I think he uses metaphor. Like when he says that he has a lamp to guide him. I don't think he really means that, really a lamp, but that he has experience that is kinda showing the way."

"He also says that there's a storm coming, but not really a storm," Shayne responded. "I think he means that the British could be like a storm coming in, and it could destroy their work."

This chapter has focused on questions that push students deeper into their analysis of the text, specifically as they explore the role of vocabulary words and phrases, text structures, and author's craft. As we have noted, not all texts need this level of scrutiny, and not all facets that explore the question *how does the text work* apply to all texts. Having said that, it is important to ensure that students have mined the inner workings of a complex text before they are required to figure out its meaning and how this text fits into a broader schema of content knowledge.

Now we invite you to test yourself. On the following page, we have included a paragraph written by Benjamin Banneker in 1791 to then–Secretary of State Thomas Jefferson; you can use this text to practice what you have learned in this chapter. In the letter, Banneker criticizes Jefferson and other framers of the Declaration of Independence for the hypocrisy "in detaining by fraud and violence so numerous a part of my brethren under groaning captivity and cruel oppression, that you should at the Same time be found guilty of that most criminal act, which you professedly detested in others, with respect to yourselves." Take a few minutes to read this text in Figure 3.6. Then turn your attention to questions that you can develop to encourage students to determine *how the text works*. Remember that this phase is focused on vocabulary, text structure, and author's craft. What is it that students should understand about the inner workings of this text before you invite them to explore what it *means*, which will be the focus of our next chapter?

Before you begin, you might like to skim the italicized questions in the teachers' lessons, above. If you'd like to check yourself, the questions that Ms. Washington developed for this text can be found on Corwin's companion website at www.corwin.com/textdependentquestions. Next, apply this technique to develop questions for a short piece that you will use with your own students.

Figure 3.6   Excerpt From Benjamin Banneker's Letter to Thomas Jefferson, August 19, 1791

This, Sir, was a time when you clearly saw into the injustice of a state of slavery, and in which you had just apprehensions of the horrors of its condition. It was now that your abhorrence thereof was so excited, that you publicly held forth this true and invaluable doctrine, which is worthy to be recorded and remembered in all succeeding ages: "We hold these truths to be self-evident, that all men are created equal; that they are endowed by their Creator with certain unalienable rights, and that among these are, life, liberty, and the pursuit of happiness." Here was a time, in which your tender feelings for yourselves had engaged you thus to declare, you were then impressed with proper ideas of the great violation of liberty, and the free possession of those blessings, to which you were entitled by nature; but, Sir, how pitiable is it to reflect, that although you were so fully convinced of the benevolence of the Father of Mankind, and of his equal and impartial distribution of these rights and privileges, which he hath conferred upon them, that you should at the same time counteract his mercies, in detaining by fraud and violence so numerous a part of my brethren, under groaning captivity and cruel oppression, that you should at the same time be found guilty of that most criminal act, which you professedly detested in others, with respect to yourselves.

Available for download from **www.corwin.com/textdependentquestions**

Videos

To read a QR code, you must have a smartphone or tablet with a camera. We recommend that you download a QR code reader app that is made specifically for your phone or tablet brand.

Videos can also be accessed at
www.corwin.com/textdependentquestions

Video 3.1 Lisa Forehand's kindergarten students talk about the word "stubby" in their vocabulary discussion based on their close read of *The Day the Crayons Quit.*

Video 3.2 Based on information in a text about cow farmers, students in Alex Cabrera's second grade class discuss the meaning of supply, demand, and inflation.

Video 3.3 Shawna Codrington's second grade class discusses the meaning of "Lon" and "Po Po" based on their reading of the Chinese folktale *Lon Po Po.*

Video 3.4 The students in Melissa Noble's fourth grade class focus on the words and phrases that the author uses to describe the characters in "Why Wisdom Is Found Everywhere."

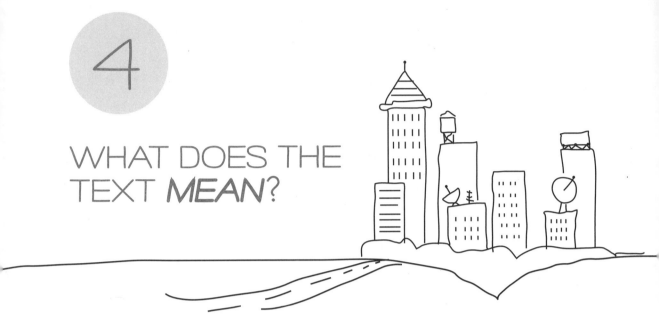

4

WHAT DOES THE TEXT *MEAN*?

The habit of reading closely begins with inspection of the text in order to develop a solid foundation in what it says—the literal meaning. It continues with investigation, as the reader analyzes the parts of the text to gain a sense of *how the text works*. But deep reading doesn't stop there. Skilled readers are able to consolidate. They see how the parts relate to the whole, and vice versa.

As humans, we interpret information in order to understand our world. We look at the sky, take note of the temperature, consider the time of year, and make a decision about whether or not we'll need an umbrella. A choreographer interprets a musical composition, giving thought to the tone and tempo, the length of the piece, and the purpose of the musical message in order to create a dance. In both cases, interpretation requires understanding the details while at the same time weighing them against the whole. Much like putting a jigsaw puzzle together, interpretation requires simultaneously looking at the pieces while imagining the whole. (Try putting a jigsaw puzzle together with the pieces turned upside down. It can be done, but it's much more difficult.)

In reading, *inferencing* is the ability to make meaning and arrive at conclusions using textual clues rather than explicitly stated information. There are several dimensions of inferencing as it applies to reading comprehension: lexical, predictive, and elaborative. Making lexical inferences requires the reader to make an informed judgment about the meaning of an ambiguous word using grammatical, contextual, and structural cues (e.g., determining whether the word *read* is a noun or verb, and whether it is past tense or present tense). Lexical inferencing is often addressed through discussion about vocabulary, which we described in detail in the previous chapter. Additionally, a reader uses her predictive inferencing skills to form a plausible hypothesis, such as whether a character reading *Frankenstein* might have trouble sleeping later that night. A third facet, elaborative inferencing, takes place when a reader fills in unstated information to provide more detail, such as imagining the way the character looked as she read a terrifying passage in Shelley's novel.

> Skilled readers are able to consolidate. They see how the parts relate to the whole, and vice versa.

All of these inferences are cognitively demanding and are not automatic. In other words, they must be nurtured. In the last chapter we spotlighted the analytic reading needed to understand the organizational parts of a text. In this chapter, we discuss how readers synthesize and interpret the parts while considering the whole piece. This is an essential step on the way to deeply understanding a text.

Three Types of Inferencing

- **Lexical:** Making an informed judgment about the meaning of an ambiguous word, using grammatical, contextual, and structural cues

- **Predictive:** Forming a plausible hypothesis

- **Elaborative:** Filling in unstated information

An Invitation to Read Closely: *Inferential*-Level Questions

We ask students inferential questions in order to gauge their ability to draw upon information that isn't stated explicitly in the text. The texts older students read require them to marshal a great deal of background knowledge about topics and concepts. Think of what these texts present as a kind of shorthand—the writer assumes a certain level of knowledge that the reader possesses. Take a look at the textbooks you used at the beginning of your teacher preparation program. It's likely that those texts were written with much more in the way of explanations of terms and practices, examples, and embedded definitions than a book about teaching that you would choose to read now. Even more important, the instructional routines discussed, now fully integrated into your professional practice, were introduced in novice terms. These textbooks were useful at the very beginning of your teaching career, but now that you are a seasoned teacher, they may no longer provide you enough nuanced information for refining your skills today.

Texts written for students who are acquiring new knowledge usually have a relatively high degree of text cohesion. Cohesion is the way text is held together. Easier texts have a high degree of cohesion in that they make cause and effect relationships explicit (*Because it rained, Sue got wet*) and they make reference to ideas, events, or objects (*Sue got wet on her way to work in the city*). Those two phrases have a high degree of cohesion at the local level, because you know where Sue was headed (to the city), why she was headed there (to work), that she got wet, and that it happened because it was raining. But any other details may need to be inferred across a longer passage. What is Sue's work, and how does she feel about it? Did she get wet because she is careless, caught by surprise, or depressed?

Now let's make it more complex. Consider any of Aesop's fables as an example of a text that is less cohesive and therefore more difficult. The major passage in each fable tells a simple story, but to reach the moral of the story, a cognitive leap has to occur. For instance, the fable "The Ant and the Grasshopper" effectively portrays two contrasting work habits, relayed using familiar narrative structures. But the final sentence says that the moral of the story is that it is better to plan ahead. There are no explanatory sentences in between the end of the story and the sentence containing the moral. For young children, the lack of connectivity (cohesion) between the main part of the story and the abstract moral presents a challenge.

Inferences are cognitively demanding and are not automatic. In other words, they must be nurtured.

Inferencing is largely dependent on one's ability to develop a cohesive thread when the author does not explicitly furnish one. It requires the reader to use background knowledge in a measured way, without going too far astray from the text. There's a lot of mental discipline needed in order to form inferences that are useful and logical but not misleading. Not every inference is a good one.

Fourth grade teacher Matt Robinson saw this happen when his students used their background knowledge a bit too vigorously during a reading of a passage about the California gold rush in 1849. While the passage primarily discussed the fact that most of the money made during this period was by those who equipped, fed, and housed the miners, the students initially wanted to focus on a single sentence that an estimated $750 million' worth of gold was discovered in a 20-year period. This information caught their attention, and when coupled with information they had read previously about a personal account of a group of early miners who struck it rich by extracting several million dollars' worth of gold in 1848, they wanted to conclude that the majority of miners were successful. The teacher used a number of prompts and cues to steer them back to the text, to no avail. "I'm hearing from many of you that you are very interested in the value of the gold," he said, "but let's look more closely. Is that enough evidence to support your conclusion that lots of miners got rich?"

Mr. Robinson recognized that in this instance, their recently developed background knowledge about the success of one group of miners trumped their ability to make textual inferences that would help them identify the central meaning of the reading. His continued instruction, including modeling and thinking aloud, assisted them in properly using both their background knowledge and the information in the text to make the correct inference about the true beneficiaries of the Gold Rush, namely the merchants who supported the miners' endeavors.

> Inferencing is largely dependent on one's ability to develop a cohesive thread when the author does not explicitly furnish one. It requires the reader to use background knowledge in a measured way, without going too far astray from the text.

Why Students Need This Type of Questioning

A stereotype about young children is that they think in simple and naïve ways. But all of us who are elementary educators know that our students are far more complex. They can be incredibly

A stereotype about young children is that they think in simple and naïve ways. But all of us who are elementary educators know that our students are far more complex.

insightful and breathtakingly wise. But when we lower our expectations about their ability to contribute to meaningful dialogue, they in turn lower their expectations about themselves. When we expect them to behave as silly beings, they oblige. We pigeonhole them at our own peril when we don't provide the forums they need to be profound; we deprive them of opportunities to experiment with ideas, to be wrong and survive the experience, to be intellectually resilient.

Using text-dependent questions that require students to synthesize and interpret information communicates to them your expectation about their cognitive capabilities. None of us intentionally pose questions to others that we don't believe they can answer. Questions that require a higher degree of cognition signal your respect for students' intellect. However, this phase of a close reading lesson serves another purpose, as it helps student build the habit of taking the time to comprehend before forming opinions. The tendency to skip over this step in order to form an uniformed opinion isn't confined to childhood. We as adults indulge in this far too often. Self-help gurus remind us to "seek first to understand, then to be understood" (Covey, 2004, p. 235). In terms of reading, Adler and Van Doren (1940/1972) call it "intellectual etiquette. . . . Do not say you agree [or] disagree . . . until you can say 'I understand'" (p. 164).

Text-dependent questions that focus on *what a text means* include those that cause readers to explore the *author's purpose* (stated or implied) and to examine them further for hidden or subversive intentions. In some cases, the writer's perspective on the topic provides insight into his or her motivation. For instance, the story in the picture book *Encounter* (Yolen, 1992) is told from the viewpoint of a Taino Indian boy on San Salvador meeting Christopher Columbus and his expedition. The author said that when she was invited to write the book, she initially thought it would be better coming from a Taino, but soon realized that the people and their culture had been wiped out. "So I said I would do it. The book was the only one in that anniversary year to speak for the Taino people in a picture book edition. It still is" (http://janeyolen.com/works/encounter, ¶1). The author casts Columbus in a different light, emphasizing the high cost paid by the native cultures he and his fellow explorers encountered. For example, the narrator says, "I watched how the sky strangers touched our golden nose rings and our golden arm-bands but not the flesh of our faces or arms. I watched their chief smile. It was a serpent's smile—no lips and all teeth." By creating a counternarrative to the more familiar histories told about explora-tion, the author provides young readers and their teachers with an opportunity to examine other viewpoints and in the process gain a more nuanced understanding of the effects of European exploration on native peoples.

The meaning of a text extends to its connection to other works. The works of writers may take on an added dimension when readers con-sider the writer's biographical information, such as examining the life of aviator Antoine de Saint-Exupéry in order to more fully under-stand *The Little Prince* (1943/2000). An informational piece on the features of the moon's surface might be further contextualized with a passage about the lunar landings during the US space program. Text-dependent questions that draw on multiple sources require students to utilize critical thinking skills to make inferences within and across texts, and to consolidate ideas and concepts learned in one or more of the disciplines.

This phase of close reading helps students build the habit of taking time to comprehend before forming opinions.

How Examining *What the Text Means* Addresses the STANDARDS

Reading Standards

The verbs used in reading **standard 7** say it all: *explain, interpret, make connections,* and *analyze.* As students solidify their understanding of *what the text says* and begin to grasp *how the text works,* they are poised to drill deeper to locate the underlying currents of the piece. Nonprint media provide an added dimension, as students are asked to apply their knowledge of multiple literacies to understand how the elements of light, sound, and motion contribute to the meaning of a literary or informational presentation. **Standard 8** is about the use of reasoning in text and therefore applies only to informational pieces. In the early grades, this means identifying points that support the author's ideas, and in the later elementary grades involves the use of evidence and text structures to support an argument. **Standard 9** expands textual knowledge by asking students to think across texts, topics, themes, and cultures. Taken together, **standards 7** and **9** outline opportunities to utilize illustration, film, texts, and audio recordings to provide students with a means to compare and contrast how a story is variously interpreted. A chart detailing the reading standards related to text meaning can be found in Figure 4.1.

Students in Lisa Forehand's kindergarten class examined the book *No, David!* (Shannon, 1998b), particularly the illustrations accompanying the sparse text. Ms. Forehand asked students to describe the characteristics of David and to provide evidence for the descriptions, drawn primarily from the illustrations. Her students said that David was "naughty" and cited evidence that he sneaks cookies from the jar and drags mud into the house. On the other hand, they made a case that he had a "good imagination" by observing that he pretended to be a pirate in his bathtub and played with his food in imaginative ways. A photograph of Ms. Forehand's language chart appears in Figure 4.2. Language charts are a visual record, often of the class conversation, that students can refer to later.

Language Standards

As discussion plays such a key role in exploring *what the text means,* the opportunities to apply the conventions of the English language are plentiful (**standard 1**). In addition, discussion of the power of language should foster students' understanding of its functions in different contexts (**standard 3**) and its vocabulary (**standard 6**). The fourth grade expectation for **standard 3** is an especially interesting one as it applies to meaning, as students make distinctions between conventions of spoken and written language.

Students in Rick Torres's class read and discussed *The Music of Dolphins* (Hesse, 1996) and the author's use of language structures to mirror the protagonist's development throughout the novel. Mila has been raised by dolphins but now has been captured and is being studied by scientists

Figure 4.1 ELA Reading Standards That Focus on *What the Text Means*

Standard (Grade)	Literary	Informational
7 (K)	With prompting and support, describe the relationship between illustrations and the story in which they appear (e.g., what moment in a story an illustration depicts).	With prompting and support, describe the relationship between illustrations and the text in which they appear (e.g., what person, place, thing, or idea in the text an illustration depicts).
7 (1)	Use illustrations and details in a story to describe its characters, setting, or events.	Use the illustrations and details in a text to describe its key ideas.
7 (2)	Use information gained from the illustrations and words in a print or digital text to demonstrate understanding of its characters, setting, or plot.	Explain how specific images (e.g., a diagram showing how a machine works) contribute to and clarify a text.
7 (3)	Explain how specific aspects of a text's illustrations contribute to what is conveyed by the words in a story (e.g., create mood, emphasize aspects of a character or setting).	Use information gained from illustrations (e.g., maps, photographs) and the words in a text to demonstrate understanding of the text (e.g., where, when, why, and how key events occur).
7 (4)	Make connections between the text of a story or drama and a visual or oral presentation of the text, identifying where each version reflects specific descriptions and directions in the text.	Interpret information presented visually, orally, or quantitatively (e.g., in charts, graphs, diagrams, time lines, animations, or interactive elements on Web pages) and explain how the information contributes to an understanding of the text in which it appears.
7 (5)	Analyze how visual and multimedia elements contribute to the meaning, tone, or beauty of a text (e.g., graphic novel, multimedia presentation of fiction, folktale, myth, poem).	Draw on information from multiple print or digital sources, demonstrating the ability to locate an answer to a question quickly or to solve a problem efficiently.
8 (K)	(Not applicable to literature)	With prompting and support, identify the reasons an author gives to support points in a text.
8 (1)	(Not applicable to literature)	Identify the reasons an author gives to support points in a text.
8 (2)	(Not applicable to literature)	Describe how reasons support specific points the author makes in a text.
8 (3)	(Not applicable to literature)	Describe the logical connection between particular sentences and paragraphs in a text (e.g., comparison, cause/effect, first/second/third in a sequence).
8 (4)	(Not applicable to literature)	Explain how an author uses reasons and evidence to support particular points in a text.

(Continued)

Figure 4.1 (Continued)

Standard (Grade)	Literary	Informational
8 (5)	(Not applicable to literature)	Explain how an author uses reasons and evidence to support particular points in a text, identifying which reasons and evidence support which point(s).
9 (K)	With prompting and support, compare and contrast the adventures and experiences of characters in familiar stories.	With prompting and support, identify basic similarities in and differences between two texts on the same topic (e.g., in illustrations, descriptions, or procedures).
9 (1)	Compare and contrast the adventures and experiences of characters in stories.	Identify basic similarities in and differences between two texts on the same topic (e.g., in illustrations, descriptions, or procedures).
9 (2)	Compare and contrast two or more versions of the same story (e.g., Cinderella stories) by different authors or from different cultures.	Compare and contrast the most important points presented by two texts on the same topic.
9 (3)	Compare and contrast the themes, settings, and plots of stories written by the same author about the same or similar characters (e.g., in books from a series).	Compare and contrast the most important points and key details presented in two texts on the same topic.
9 (4)	Compare and contrast the treatment of similar themes and topics (e.g., opposition of good and evil) and patterns of events (e.g., the quest) in stories, myths, and traditional literature from different cultures.	Integrate information from two texts on the same topic in order to write or speak about the subject knowledgeably.
9 (5)	Compare and contrast stories in the same genre (e.g., mysteries and adventure stories) on their approaches to similar themes and topics.	Integrate information from several texts on the same topic in order to write or speak about the subject knowledgeably.
10 (K)	Actively engage in group reading activities with purpose and understanding.	
10 (1)	With prompting and support, read prose and poetry of appropriate complexity for grade 1.	With prompting and support, read informational texts appropriately complex for grade 1.
10 (2)	By the end of the year, read and comprehend literature, including stories and poetry, in the grades 2–3 text complexity band proficiently, with scaffolding as needed at the high end of the range.	By the end of year, read and comprehend informational texts, including history/social studies, science, and technical texts, in the grades 2–3 text complexity band proficiently, with scaffolding as needed at the high end of the range.
10 (3)	By the end of the year, read and comprehend literature, including stories, dramas, and poetry, at the high end of the grades 2–3 text complexity band independently and proficiently.	By the end of the year, read and comprehend informational texts, including history/social studies, science, and technical texts, at the high end of the grades 2–3 text complexity band independently and proficiently.

Standard (Grade)	Literary	Informational
10 (4)	By the end of the year, read and comprehend literature, including stories, dramas, and poetry, in the grades 4–5 text complexity band proficiently, with scaffolding as needed at the high end of the range.	By the end of year, read and comprehend informational texts, including history/social studies, science, and technical texts, in the grades 4–5 text complexity band proficiently, with scaffolding as needed at the high end of the range.
10 (5)	By the end of the year, read and comprehend literature, including stories, dramas, and poetry, at the high end of the grades 4–5 text complexity band independently and proficiently.	By the end of the year, read and comprehend informational texts, including history/social studies, science, and technical texts, at the high end of the grades 4–5 text complexity band independently and proficiently.

Figure 4.2   Language Chart for *No, David!*

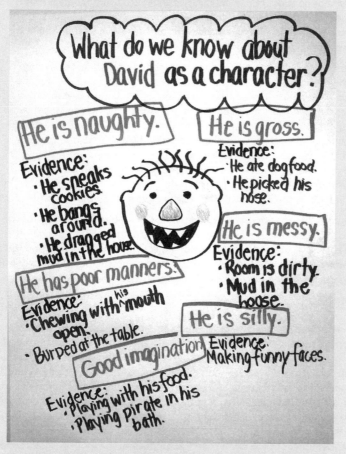

to learn about arrested development in humans. "My students notice right away that the main narrative is told in simple sentences, while Mila's thoughts, which are in italics, involve more complex language structures," he said. "In addition to the story, we talk about the gap between what Mila feels and what she can express in her speech. It makes for some great conversation about the meaning of the text and how we experience her inner conflict." A table displaying these targeted language standards can be found in Figure 4.3.

Speaking and Listening Standards

The standards are replete with opportunities for expanding speaking and listening skills through extended discussion, and **standards 1, 4,** and **6** have been reviewed in previous chapters. But **standards 2** and **3** are of particular note in the context of determining text meaning. (Figure 4.4 lists the grade-specific speaking and listening standards.)

Standard 2 in speaking and listening aligns with reading **standard 7**'s emphasis on using diverse texts, media, and visual displays. To be clear, analysis of nonprint media is similar to analysis of print media (*What does the text say? How does the text work?*), but we have chosen to spotlight diverse formats in this chapter precisely because these often offer a path for further contextualizing content.

After a long winter that seemed to never end, spring finally came to the northwestern community where Jayla Lewis and her third grade students live. In preparation for the inevitable arrival of spring, Ms. Lewis video recorded adults at her school reciting the poem "After the Winter" by Claude McKay (www .poetryfoundation.org/poem/237358). On the first warm day, she played a video that included readings of the poem by the children's principal, school secretary, and custodian as well as some of their teachers and a parent. The students read the poem in print and discussed its meaning, especially in visualizing the "summer isle" the poet described, and located photographs that illustrated the poem. (We will explore this project in more detail in Chapter 5.)

Standard 3 in speaking and listening offers more direction on the role of logic and reasoning. In the same way that reading **standard 8** requires students to locate and analyze reasoning within a text, speaking and listening **standard 3** requires effective speakers and listeners to adhere to a logical progression in their discussions. While **standard 4** (discussed in previous chapters) reflects the demands on the speaker, **standard 3** asks students to use their listening skills to detect when and where these demands occur.

Hannah Johnstone's first grade science students are studying the patterns of animal parental behavior that help animal babies survive. They view a National Geographic Kids two-minute video several times. The video shows wood duck babies as they hatch and then take their first plunge into the water. The narrator describes their 15-foot jump from the nest as "the big ordeal." He then asks about the courage of baby ducks and states that if the ducks fail to jump, they will starve. Ms. Johnstone and her students list the visual and narrative information that supports the description of the big ordeal, the courageousness of the ducks, and the purpose of the mother duck's behavior.

Figure 4.3 Language Standards That Focus on *What the Text Means*

	Kindergarten	Grade 1	Grade 2	Grade 3	Grade 4	Grade 5
1	Demonstrate command of the conventions of standard English grammar and usage when writing or speaking.	Demonstrate command of the conventions of standard English grammar and usage when writing or speaking.	Demonstrate command of the conventions of standard English grammar and usage when writing or speaking.	Demonstrate command of the conventions of standard English grammar and usage when writing or speaking.	Demonstrate command of the conventions of standard English grammar and usage when writing or speaking.	Demonstrate command of the conventions of standard English grammar and usage when writing or speaking.
	a. Print many upper- and lowercase letters.	a. Print all upper- and lowercase letters.	a. Use collective nouns (e.g., *group*).	a. Explain the function of nouns, pronouns, verbs, adjectives, and adverbs in general and their functions in particular sentences.	a. Use relative pronouns (*who, whose, whom, which, that*) and relative adverbs (*where, when, why*).	a. Explain the function of conjunctions, prepositions, and interjections in general and their function in particular sentences.
	b. Use frequently occurring nouns and verbs.	b. Use common, proper, and possessive nouns.	b. Form and use frequently occurring irregular plural nouns (e.g., *feet, children, teeth, mice, fish*).	b. Form and use regular and irregular plural nouns.	b. Form and use the progressive (e.g., *I was walking; I am walking; I will be walking*) verb tenses.	b. Form and use the perfect (e.g., *I had walked; I have walked; I will have walked*) verb tenses.
	c. Form regular plural nouns orally by adding /s/ or /es/ (e.g., *dog, dogs; wish, wishes*).	c. Use singular and plural nouns with matching verbs in basic sentences (e.g., *He hops; We hop*).	c. Use reflexive pronouns (e.g., *myself, ourselves*).	c. Use abstract nouns (e.g., *childhood*).	c. Use modal auxiliaries (e.g., *can, may, must*) to convey various conditions.	c. Use verb tense to convey various times, sequences, states, and conditions.
	d. Understand and use question words (interrogatives) (e.g., *who, what, where, when, why, how*).	d. Use personal, possessive, and indefinite pronouns (e.g., *I, me, my; they, them, their; anyone, everything*).	d. Form and use the past tense of frequently occurring irregular verbs (e.g., *sat, hid, told*).	d. Form and use regular and irregular verbs.	d. Order adjectives within sentences according to conventional patterns (e.g., *a small red bag* rather than *a red small bag*).	d. Recognize and correct inappropriate shifts in verb tense.
	e. Use the most frequently occurring prepositions (e.g., *to, from, in, out, on, off, for, of, by, with*).	e. Use verbs to convey a sense of past, present, and future (e.g., *Yesterday I walked home; Today I walk home; Tomorrow I will walk home*).	e. Use adjectives and adverbs, and choose between them depending on what is to be modified.	e. Form and use the simple (e.g., *I walked; I walk; I will walk*) verb tenses.		
				f. Ensure subject-verb and pronoun-antecedent agreement.		

(Continued)

Figure 4.3 (Continued)

	Kindergarten	Grade 1	Grade 2	Grade 3	Grade 4	Grade 5
	f. Produce and expand complete sentences in shared language activities.	f. Use frequently occurring adjectives. g. Use frequently occurring conjunctions (e.g., *and, but, or, so, because*). h. Use determiners (e.g., articles, demonstratives). i. Use frequently occurring prepositions (e.g., *during, beyond, toward*). j. Produce and expand complete simple and compound declarative, interrogative, imperative, and exclamatory sentences in response to prompts.	f. Produce, expand, and rearrange complete simple and compound sentences (e.g., *The boy watched the movie; The little boy watched the movie; The action movie was watched by the little boy*).	g. Form and use comparative and superlative adjectives and adverbs, and choose between them depending on what is to be modified. h. Use coordinating and subordinating conjunctions. i. Produce simple, compound, and complex sentences.	e. Form and use prepositional phrases. f. Produce complete sentences, recognizing and correcting inappropriate fragments and run-ons. g. Correctly use frequently confused words (e.g., *to, too, two; there, their*).	e. Use correlative conjunctions (e.g., *either/or, neither/nor*).
3	(Begins in grade 2)	(Begins in grade 2)	Use knowledge of language and its conventions when writing, speaking, reading, or listening.	Use knowledge of language and its conventions when writing, speaking, reading, or listening.	Use knowledge of language and its conventions when writing, speaking, reading, or listening.	Use knowledge of language and its conventions when writing, speaking, reading, or listening.

Kindergarten	Grade 1	Grade 2	Grade 3	Grade 4	Grade 5
		a. Compare formal and informal uses of English.	a. Choose words and phrases for effect. b. Recognize and observe differences between the conventions of spoken and written standard English.	a. Choose words and phrases to convey ideas precisely. b. Choose punctuation for effect. c. Differentiate between contexts that call for formal English (e.g., presenting ideas) and situations where informal discourse is appropriate (e.g., small-group discussion).	a. Expand, combine, and reduce sentences for meaning, reader/listener interest, and style. b. Compare and contrast the varieties of English (e.g., dialects, registers) used in stories, dramas, or poems.
6 Use words and phrases acquired through conversations, reading and being read to, and responding to texts.	Use words and phrases acquired through conversations, reading and being read to, and responding to texts, including using frequently occurring conjunctions to signal simple relationships (e.g., because).	Use words and phrases acquired through conversations, reading and being read to, and responding to texts, including using adjectives and adverbs to describe (e.g., When other kids are happy that makes me happy).	Acquire and use accurately grade-appropriate conversational, general academic, and domain specific words and phrases, including those that signal spatial and temporal relationships (e.g., After dinner that night we went looking for them).	Acquire and use accurately grade-appropriate general academic and domain-specific words and phrases, including those that signal precise actions, emotions, or states of being (e.g., quizzed, whined, stammered) and that are basic to a particular topic (e.g., wildlife, conservation, and endangered when discussing animal preservation).	Acquire and use accurately grade-appropriate general academic and domain-specific words and phrases, including those that signal contrast, addition, and other logical relationships (e.g., however, although, nevertheless, similarly, moreover, in addition).

Figure 4.4 Speaking and Listening Standards That Focus on *What the Text Means*

	Kindergarten	Grade 1	Grade 2	Grade 3	Grade 4	Grade 5
1	Participate in collaborative conversations with diverse partners about *kindergarten topics and texts* with peers and adults in small and larger groups.	Participate in collaborative conversations with diverse partners about *grade 1 topics and texts* with peers and adults in small and larger groups.	Participate in collaborative conversations with diverse partners about *grade 2 topics and texts* with peers and adults in small and larger groups.	Engage effectively in a range of collaborative discussions (one-on-one, in groups, and teacher-led) with diverse partners on *grade 3 topics and texts*, building on others' ideas and expressing their own clearly.	Engage effectively in a range of collaborative discussions (one-on-one, in groups, and teacher-led) with diverse partners on *grade 4 topics and texts*, building on others' ideas and expressing their own clearly.	Engage effectively in a range of collaborative discussions (one-on-one, in groups, and teacher-led) with diverse partners on *grade 5 topics and texts*, building on others' ideas and expressing their own clearly.
	a. Follow agreed-upon rules for discussions (e.g., listening to others and taking turns speaking about the topics and texts under discussion).	a. Follow agreed-upon rules for discussions (e.g., listening to others with care, speaking one at a time about the topics and texts under discussion).	a. Follow agreed-upon rules for discussions (e.g., gaining the floor in respectful ways, listening to others with care, speaking one at a time about the topics and texts under discussion).	a. Come to discussions prepared, having read or studied required material; explicitly draw on that preparation and other information known about the topic to explore ideas under discussion.	a. Come to discussions prepared, having read or studied required material; explicitly draw on that preparation and other information known about the topic to explore ideas under discussion.	a. Come to discussions prepared, having read or studied required material; explicitly draw on that preparation and other information known about the topic to explore ideas under discussion.
	b. Continue a conversation through multiple exchanges.	b. Build on others' talk in conversations by responding to the comments of others through multiple exchanges.	b. Build on others' talk in conversations by linking their comments to the remarks of others.	b. Follow agreed-upon rules for discussions (e.g., gaining the floor in respectful ways, listening	b. Follow agreed-upon rules for discussions and carry out assigned roles.	b. Follow agreed-upon rules for discussions and carry out assigned roles.
		c. Ask questions to clear up any confusion about the topics and texts under discussion.	c. Ask for clarification and further explanation as needed about the topics and texts under discussion.		c. Pose and respond	c. Pose and respond

	Kindergarten	Grade 1	Grade 2	Grade 3	Grade 4	Grade 5
				to others with care, speaking one at a time about the topics and texts under discussion). c. Ask questions to check understanding of information presented, stay on topic, and link their comments to the remarks of others. d. Explain their own ideas and understanding in light of the discussion.	to specific questions to clarify or follow up on information, and make comments that contribute to the discussion and link to the remarks of others. d. Review the key ideas expressed and explain their own ideas and understanding in light of the discussion.	to specific questions by making comments that contribute to the discussion and elaborate on the remarks of others. d. Review the key ideas expressed and draw conclusions in light of information and knowledge gained from the discussions.
2	Confirm understanding of a text read aloud or information presented orally or through other media by asking and answering questions about key details and requesting clarification if something is not understood.	Ask and answer questions about key details in a text read aloud or information presented orally or through other media.	Recount or describe key ideas or details from a text read aloud or information presented orally or through other media.	Determine the main ideas and supporting details of a text read aloud or information presented in diverse media and formats, including visually, quantitatively, and orally.	Paraphrase portions of a text read aloud or information presented in diverse media and formats, including visually, quantitatively, and orally.	Summarize a written text read aloud or information presented in diverse media and formats, including visually, quantitatively, and orally.

(Continued)

Figure 4.4 (Continued)

	Kindergarten	Grade 1	Grade 2	Grade 3	Grade 4	Grade 5
3	Ask and answer questions in order to seek help, get information, or clarify something that is not understood.	Ask and answer questions about what a speaker says in order to gather additional information or clarify something that is not understood.	Ask and answer questions about what a speaker says in order to clarify comprehension, gather additional information, or deepen understanding of a topic or issue.	Ask and answer questions about information from a speaker, offering appropriate elaboration and detail.	Identify the reasons and evidence a speaker provides to support particular points.	Summarize the points a speaker makes and explain how each claim is supported by reasons and evidence.
4	Describe familiar people, places, things, and events and, with prompting and support, provide additional detail.	Describe people, places, things, and events with relevant details, expressing ideas and feelings clearly.	Tell a story or recount an experience with appropriate facts and relevant, descriptive details, speaking audibly in coherent sentences.	Report on a topic or text, tell a story, or recount an experience with appropriate facts and relevant, descriptive details, speaking clearly at an understandable pace.	Report on a topic or text, tell a story, or recount an experience in an organized manner, using appropriate facts and relevant, descriptive details to support main ideas or themes; speak clearly at an understandable pace.	Report on a topic or text or present an opinion, sequencing ideas logically and using appropriate facts and relevant, descriptive details to support main ideas or themes; speak clearly at an understandable pace.
6	Speak audibly and express thoughts, feelings, and ideas clearly.	Produce complete sentences when appropriate to task and situation.	Produce complete sentences when appropriate to task and situation in order to provide requested detail or clarification.	Speak in complete sentences when appropriate to task and situation in order to provide requested detail or clarification.	Differentiate between contexts that call for formal English (e.g., presenting ideas) and situations where informal discourse is appropriate (e.g., small-group discussion); use formal English when appropriate to task and situation.	Adapt speech to a variety of contexts and tasks, using formal English when appropriate to task and situation.

Using Text-Dependent Questions
About *What the Text Means*

As noted in previous chapters, the text-dependent questions we develop in advance of a discussion can ensure that students' awareness of a text's meaning deepens over time. As we move beyond questions about vocabulary and text structure and locating explicitly stated information, we transition students into a heavier reliance on inferences. They are further challenged to use evidence and reasoning in their discussions. Because of this, lessons about *what the text means* may take longer and will be punctuated by periods of silence as students think closely. You may discover that you're only posing a few of these questions, because it takes students longer to draw conclu-

We always view those moments when students stop talking to us and begin talking to one another as a sign of success.

sions. Our experience is that this phase of instruction results in longer student responses and more conversation across the room. We always view those moments when students stop talking to us and begin talking to one another as a sign of success.

Understanding a text more deeply allows students to make logical inferences from the text. Authors *imply* and readers *infer*. To infer, students must understand the author's purpose and how a given text relates to other texts. In the following sections, we focus on helping students figure out *what the text means* by attending to two main elements of texts:

- Author's purpose

- Intertextual connections

But inferencing doesn't end there. In Chapter 5, we focus our attention on students' use of the text to accomplish other tasks. It's in this fourth phase that logical inferences that include text evidence are realized.

Questions for Determining the Author's Purpose

Writers write for a host of reasons. Some of these reasons—to convey an experience, to inform or explain, and to argue a position—parallel the three major text types. When we pose text-dependent questions about the author's purpose, we don't purport to delve into the deep psychological motivations of the writer. But we do examine the text carefully for stated purposes and seek to contextualize the writing using what we know about the time and circumstances of its creation. It is helpful when the writer states, "The purpose of the study was to . . . ," because it makes the process more transparent. Statements such as this typically appear in scientific research articles but rarely appear outside of these documents. Instead, as is often the case in narrative texts, the reader usually has to dig around a bit more to glean this information. The author's purpose can often be inferred through examination of several features of the text. Below are three ways you can teach students to do this.

> Lessons about *what the text means* may take longer and will be punctuated by periods of silence as students think closely.

Consider Bias. Each writer shines a unique light on a topic, and with that comes a unique set of biases. Biases are not inherently negative; our attitudes, experiences, and perspectives are what make all of us interesting. In the case of some texts, the bias is inconsequential. For instance, an informational text explaining the lifecycle of a frog is probably not going to offer much at all in the way of bias. Alternatively, the informational text *Plastic Ahoy! Investigating the Great Pacific Garbage Patch* (Newman, 2014) has a strong author's bias about the damage humans are doing to the sea. The author's point of view is less important in a text like *The Hunger Games* (Collins, 2010), but it could influence understanding in a narrative text that is based on experiences an author has had, as is the case in *Stuck in Neutral* (Trueman, 2000), a text told from the perspective of an adolescent who has a significant disability and believes his father wants to kill him. In the latter case, the author notes that he wrote the book because of a lawsuit in Canada and his own experience as the parent of a child with a disability.

Identify the Format. A blog post cannot be understood solely for its content; it must also be understood through the platform, in this case, the Internet. That author's purpose is further contextualized based on the hosting website. Does the post appear on the website of a respected organization or on one with a poor reputation? Printed text deserves the same inspection. Does it appear in a well-regarded magazine, or is it featured in a publication underwritten by a special interest group? Similarly, a poem must be analyzed in the format in which it was produced, which would differ from that of a short story or memoir.

Consider How the Author Wants the Reader to React. Every written and verbal communication contains the rhetoric of human thought. The Greek philosopher Aristotle described three modes of rhetoric as methods of persuasion:

- *Ethos* appeals to the credibility of the writer or speaker, including his or her likability, authority, and character.

- *Pathos* appeals to the emotions of the listener or reader.

- *Logos* appeals to formal reasoning and logic, including inductive and deductive reasoning, and the use of facts and statistics.

We do not ask elementary school students to consciously identify the use of these modes of persuasion in the texts they read. Instead, we focus on opinions: the opinions of the author and the opinions that can be drawn from the text itself. As students learn to analyze texts in this way, they begin to incorporate these modes in their own writing.

Questions for Determining the
Author's Purpose in Kindergarten and First Grade

The students in Mr. Bradley's class had discussed a great deal about the text, *Winnie-the-Pooh* (Milne, 1926), but they had not discussed the purpose of the text. As students learn to read and discuss texts, they need to consider the various reasons that the text was written. Mr. Bradley wanted his students to learn that they read some texts to become informed about a topic, other texts to perform a task, and still other texts purely for enjoyment. To reinforce this, he directly asked his students why they thought authors wrote specific texts.

While reading *Winnie-the-Pooh*, Mr. Bradley asked his students, *"Why do you suppose Mr. Milne wrote this?* We didn't talk about this question in Chapter 1 because we wanted to get into the book a little more. Now we're ready. *What was the author's purpose in writing this book? Was it to teach us something, like how to get bears out of holes? Or to help us with a task, like having company over? Or was it to entertain us?"*

A teacher checks in on groups discussing the question.

"It's just fun," Michael said. "It's a story for fun. But sometimes you can learn stuff from stories too."

Mr. Bradley responded, "I think you're right. There are things that we can learn from stories. We call those life lessons, lessons that help you live a better life. Like when we read *Chrysanthemum* (Henkes, 1991) and agreed that every name for every person was wonderful. So that does happen, right? But the author's purpose for *Winnie-the-Pooh* is mainly to make us smile, to entertain us, right?"

Questions for Determining the
Author's Purpose in Second and Third Grades

The students had found evidence of tone in the character analyses of the ant and the boy in *Hey, Little Ant* (Hoose & Hoose, 1998) as they discussed author's craft, which made the transition to author's purpose seamless. *"So why would this father and daughter write this? What do they hope to accomplish?"* Ms. Perez asked them.

"That's easy," Joseph said, turning to his group. "To stop kids from killing all of the ants. I saw that on the playground. There was fifth graders smashing the ants over by the bars."

"Yeah, not to kill ants," Sabrina said. "And maybe not to hurt other animals."

Listening to the groups discuss the question, Ms. Perez realized that they had missed the deeper meaning of the text. Her students were focused on a fairly literal interpretation of the text and specifically of the author's purpose. She interrupted the groups, asking a new question.

"I wonder if the authors want their readers to take action on a grander scale. What if this isn't about ants and boys, really? What if they intended for you to learn a lesson? What lesson could that be? And make sure you discuss the evidence that leads your conclusions."

For several minutes the groups discussed the deeper meanings in the text. Slowly, they came to realize that the text was about peer pressure and bullying. As Juan said to his group, "So, now I think maybe it was about being a bully. Like, the boy could hurt the ant. But is that the right thing to do? Like we are supposed to think about is it right to hurt somebody because we're bigger than them? I think that is what Ms. Perez is thinking about."

"I think you're right," Sarah responded, "because the pictures make him look like a bully. But also, the friends want him to squish the ant. They're saying to do it. Like it says 'they all say I **should** squish you.' Like a fight when the other kids make it worse. They're just trying to make him do something that maybe he doesn't want to do."

In bringing the class back together, Ms. Perez asked, *"How many of you are talking about bullying?* I heard that in a lot of groups. [lots of hands go up] And what else? I heard groups talking about the friends and their role. *The author had a purpose, and each page is important in our understanding.* Marlon, what did your group say?"

"We kinda said that it was peer pressure, like we talked about at the assembly. You don't have to do something just because other people are doing it. Or because they tell you to do it. That's peer pressure. It can make you do something you don't really want to do."

Questions for Determining the
Author's Purpose in Fourth and Fifth Grades

The students in Ms. Washington's class were very aware of the purpose for the Patrick Henry speech. They understood that the author intended to gain support for fighting with the British. They understood that the speech contained a lot of evidence to support his point and that he used a number of literary devices to convince his listeners that he was right. Now they were ready to tackle some deeper messages in the text. Ms. Washington started this deeper investigation of the text by asking them about a line that they had previously discussed.

"I'd like us to go back to a line in the text that we talked about before. It says, 'Is life so dear, or peace so weak, as to be purchased at the price of chains and slavery?' We know that he made reference to slavery earlier in the text. Why did Patrick Henry include the threat of slavery in his speech? What was the purpose, and how do you know?"

As the groups talked, they seemed to focus on the idea that slavery was feared, that the people in the room did not want to be treated like they had seen slaves being treated.

"So, maybe it's the worst thing he could think of as punishment that the British could do to the colonists. He even says that they are going to put them in chains," Marissa said.

"I totally agree," David added. "It's like he's saying, if we don't do something to try to win, then they can conquer us like they did to other people. That's what I think."

Questions for Making Intertextual Connections

Texts don't exist in isolation; they are better understood when compared and contrasted with other texts, including those that utilize other media platforms, such as audio recordings, film, and multimedia. In the case of diverse media applications, the target text may be better understood when images are used to augment description. This is often the case with texts that were written long ago and with stories that occur in unfamiliar settings. Fourth grade teacher Matt Robinson used film clips to provide his students with a visual vocabulary that supported their readings about historical events. "It's amazing how much it helps when I use a short clip from a documentary about a time in history," he said. "We're studying the Gold Rush right now, and the textbook has some great photographs for them to view. But I've discovered that a short, well-done reenactment gives them so much more," commented Mr. Robinson. "It helps them understand unique elements of the time, like the fact that most people walked or rode a horse to get from one place to another. [My students] see that people from long ago have much in common with themselves, like the need to move from one place to another, and that the rich usually have a better ride than the poor."

Intertextual connections are necessary in order for students to translate and integrate information. For instance, in social studies,

> The target text may be better understood when images are used to augment description. This is often the case with texts that were written long ago and with stories that occur in unfamiliar settings.

students must discern the difference between primary and secondary source documents and recognize the benefits and drawbacks of each. The details and perspective of an eyewitness account can round out understanding of an event, such as the use of photographs from *Lincoln: A Photobiography* (Freedman, 1987). Of course, the photographs don't provide the context and details. Only a secondary source, such as their textbook or another informational piece, would be able to do so. Each is of value; both become more valuable when used together.

In science, students translate quantitative and visual data into words, and vice versa. Words and images that enable them to make these translations may be found inside of a single text, such as when a chart or diagram is used to represent a complex process. For example, an informational reading on the lifecycle of a butterfly is likely to contain a diagram that details the process. In addition, the diagram will likely indicate the names of each stage and the order in which the process occurs. The accompanying written text will contain more information about the details of the process and an explanation. The diagram and textual information are best understood in conjunction with one another, and each has its own demands. In the diagram, color features, the caption, directionality arrows, and a scale provide visual representations of information. Text-dependent questions about what the diagram means include those that ask students to interpret information and to describe the process. Questions that foster discussion about elaborative inferencing within scientific diagrams increase student comprehension in biology (Cromley et al., 2013).

A final dimension for intertextual connections involves the ways in which literary texts are performed across platforms. A common example of this exists in virtually every classroom: the practice of video viewing. Videos are widely available and provide students with visual information that is difficult to capture with words alone. In close reading, videos should be used later in the process, when students have a reasonably strong understanding of *what the text says* and *what the text means*. Other resources include audio recordings of speeches, and organizations such as the National Archives (www.archives.gov) and the Library of Congress (www .loc.gov) are invaluable for locating these and other multimedia materials.

Mr. Bradley had read Chapter 2 from *Winnie-the-Pooh* to his students twice. They had a number of powerful conversations about the text that allowed them to practice their listening and thinking skills. But he also wanted them to practice comparing versions of texts, so he showed them a clip (2 minutes 32 seconds) from the movie *Mini Adventures of Winnie the Pooh* (https://www.youtube .com/watch?v=UDm3NlSSJyg). This Disney version contained the same essential plot and character elements but differed in a number of ways.

After they had finished watching the clip, Mr. Bradley said, *"Let's compare the versions of this story. What was the same and what was different?"*

The students started talking excitedly. Chase and Kiara, for example, focused on the beginning, saying, "Rabbit didn't pretend not to be home. He just went to visit his friend."

Michael and Hunter talked about the use of Pooh's backside. "Rabbit made a picture with his butt. Then he sneezed and it flew all over. The book said his feet was towels."

Brian and Angela noted that when Pooh got unstuck, he flew into the air and got stuck in a tree.

Bringing his students back together, Mr. Bradley said, "Let's make a chart to compare the things that were the same and the things that were different. I'll start. I noticed one thing that was the same. Winnie-the-Pooh was stuck in a hole. Who wants to share one?"

"I noticed one thing that was the same," Brittany said. "Winnie-the-Pooh was at Rabbit's house."

"I noticed one thing that was different," Christine said. "Christopher Robin did not read to him."

"I noticed one thing that was the same: Winnie-the-Pooh was eating honey," said Brian.

"I noticed one thing that was different," Zoe said. "Kangaroo came to visit."

Questions for Making Intertextual
Connections in Second and Third Grades

Ms. Perez wanted her students to understand the impact of peer pressure, which was one of her primary goals in introducing her students to *Hey, Little Ant* (Hoose & Hoose, 1998). Following their discussion about the author's purpose, Ms. Perez read the text *A Bad Case of Stripes* (Shannon, 1998a). This story focuses on a girl who does not eat her lima beans, even though she loves them, because other kids at school don't like them.

Ms. Perez read the text aloud once and asked her students, "Please take turns retelling the text to your group. Try to tell the story in order." Following this short task, Ms. Perez said to her students, "*Let's compare these two books.* They both involve peer pressure, that's obvious. That's not my question. *My question is how does each character respond to the peer pressure?*"

Javier informed his group that there were big differences. "The boy in the ant book didn't respond at all. The author makes you decide. In the stripe book, the girl has to eat the beans to be normal again."

"So, it's easier to do something when you really have to, like the girl did," Sarah said. "It's harder when you have to decide for yourself."

Ms. Perez wanted to arm her students with some information about peer pressure, so the next day she invited them to read a short informational text from the Kid's HelpLine website (http://www .kidshelp.com.au/kids/information/hot-topics/peer-pressure.php). "Please take out your iPads and click on the link I saved for you. Take a few minutes to read over this text and then we'll come back together. You can also turn on the voice, if you want, and have it read aloud."

A few minutes later, she asked, "*Now that you have read the article, I'd like you to talk about the type of peer pressure each of our characters experienced: spoken or unspoken?*"

Listening in on her students, Ms. Perez noted that they fully grasped this information. They correctly noted that the boy experienced spoken pressure, and the girl experienced unspoken pressure. She then turned their attention to the actions of the characters, saying, "Take a look again at the section called 'Standing up to peer pressure.' *What did our characters do? And what advice could you give our characters based on this information?"*

"The boy didn't really do any of these," Marlon said, "but I think he should know hisself. If you know what you believe, then it wouldn't matter if his friends wanted him to do something, like squash those ants."

"I think that the girl thought about the consequences and made a decision," Christine said, speaking up from another group. "But maybe she could also think ahead so that at lunch she could be ready if she was going to do something that wasn't so popular but was important to her."

Questions for Making Intertextual
Connections in Fourth and Fifth Grades

Ms. Washington wanted to make sure that her students understood the course of action following Patrick Henry's speech. Based on her experience teaching fifth graders about the American Revolution, she knew that a common misconception was that fighting with the British immediately took place following this historic oration.

The first source she asked her students to review was the resolution that was passed following Patrick Henry's speech (see Figure 4.5). Knowing that this text was very complex, Ms. Washington read it aloud to her students after they read it independently. She then asked, *"I'm looking for the big idea here. What did the Virginia legislature decide to do?"*

"I don't get the whole thing, but I think that they created an army," Mariah said. "I think militia is like the military. The words are practically the same, and they want to fight, so it makes sense."

"I agree with you," Jessie said, "because my dad says the word *militia* when he watches the news about wars in other places. And I think it was in our social studies book, when they made the army, right?"

Ms. Washington interrupted the groups, knowing that her students understood the action taken following Patrick Henry's speech. She wanted them to understand that the resolution did not have unanimous support and that it took some time before the war started

**Figure 4.5   Resolutions of the Provincial Congress
of Virginia; March 23, 1775**

Resolved, that a well regulated militia composed of gentlemen and yeomen is the natural strength and only security of a free government; that such a militia in this colony would forever render it unnecessary for the mother country to keep among us, for the purpose of our defence, any standing army of mercenary forces, always subversive of the quiet, and dangerous to the liberties of the people, and would obviate the pretext of taxing us for their support.

That the establishment of such a militia is at this time peculiarly necessary, by the state of our laws for the protection and defence of the country some of which have already expired, and others will shortly do so; and that the known remissness of government in calling us together in a legislative capacity renders it too insecure in this time of danger and distress, to rely that opportunity will be given of renewing them in General Assembly or making any provision to secure our inestimable rights and liberties from those farther violations with which they are threatened.

Resolved therefore, that this colony be immediately put into a posture of defence: and that Patrick Henry, Richard Henry Lee, Robert Carter Nicholas, Benjamin Harrison, Lemuel Riddick, George Washington, Adam Stephen, Andrew Lewis, William Christian, Edmund Pendleton, Thomas Jefferson and Isaac Zane, Esquires, be a committee to prepare a plan for the embodying arming and disciplining such a number of men as may be sufficient for that purpose.

and even longer before the Declaration of Independence was drafted. She showed the clip (3 minutes 45 seconds) titled "Virginia's Response to Patrick Henry's Resolution" (http://classroomclips.org/video/842).

Following presentation of this second source, Ms. Washington asked her students, *"How did various people respond to Patrick Henry's speech?"* Her students talked with each other about the fact that not everyone supported the motion.

"I was surprised," Wendy said. "I thought that they would all vote for Patrick Henry after his speech. But there were lots of people who didn't want to fight with Britain."

"And it even said that it barely passed," Noah added. "Could you imagine if it didn't pass? It would be totally different now."

"The committee was interesting, because there were people on it that didn't agree," Kevin said. "I thought that they would only put people on the committee who voted yes. But that was probably a good idea, like it said, so that they could get more support before the war started."

Ms. Washington was pleased with her students' response and knew that they were gaining a better understanding of the context and history of the American Revolution. Before leaving this text, she said to her students, who were working in groups to learn more about an assigned colony:

> Remember, this is only Virginia. There are other colonies. Only one group represents Virginia. You have to think about how the people in your colony might respond to this information. There were loyalists, free and enslaved African Americans, and patriots in each colony. And that's what we really need to think about. How is each colony going to react to this?

> Before we end, I want to show you an image that Benjamin Franklin created (see Figure 4.6). Take a look at this.

> This was the very first ever political cartoon, published in 1754, way before Patrick Henry gave his speech. In fact, this wasn't even about the British. It was Franklin's statement that the colonies were not united and that they couldn't reach agreement about wars with the French and Native Americans. But this image became very popular just before and during the American Revolution. Why do you think that is the case?

"Look, it's all cut up, like it can't get together," Shayne said. "That's what happened in the colonies before the American Revolution. They couldn't agree."

Figure 4.6 Benjamin Franklin's Political Cartoon, May 9, 1754

"I noticed that they are in order, from the north down, like on a map," Zoe added. "He drew them in the order of the colonies at that time. And Virginia has a twist, so maybe they were really confused or really important."

"I think he's saying if we don't get together, we will die," Marcus said. "If you cut up the snake like that, then it will die. That's what Patrick Henry was saying in his speech. That if they don't fight, they will become slaves to the British or that they will all be dead if they don't agree to do what the king says."

·QUESTION YOURSELF

This chapter has focused on questions that push students even deeper into their analysis of the text, specifically as they explore the role of inferences, author's purpose, and intertextual connections. These deep analyses of texts are possible when students know *what the text says* and *how the text works*.

Now we invite you to test yourself. In Figure 4.7 we have included an article about the 1854 London cholera epidemic that you can use to practice what you have learned in this chapter. Take a few minutes to read the text below. Then turn your attention to the questions that you can develop to encourage students to determine *what the text means*. Remember that this phase is focused on making *inferences* and specifically understanding *author's purpose* and *intertextual connections*. What is it that students should understand about this text? How might the data table on the page that follows, or the map that follows that, help them understand the text?

Before you begin, you might like to skim the italicized questions in the teachers' lessons, above. If you'd like to check yourself, the questions that Ms. Thayre developed can be found on Corwin's companion website at www.corwin.com/textdependentquestions. Next, apply this technique to develop questions for a short piece that you will use with your own students.

Figure 4.7 **"Instances of the Communication of Cholera Through the Medium of Polluted Water in the Neighborhood of Broad Street, Golden Square" by John Snow**

The most terrible outbreak of cholera which ever occurred in this kingdom, is probably that which took place in Broad Street, Golden Square, and the adjoining streets, a few weeks ago. Within two hundred and fifty yards of the spot where Cambridge Street joins Broad Street, there were upwards of five hundred fatal attacks of cholera in ten days. The mortality in this limited area probably equals any that was ever caused in this country, even by the plague; and it was much more sudden, as the greater number of cases terminated in a few hours. The mortality would undoubtedly have been much greater had it not been for the flight of the population. Persons in furnished lodgings left first, then other lodgers went away, leaving their furniture to be sent for when they could meet with a place to put it in. Many houses were closed altogether, owing to the death of the proprietors; and, in a great number of instances, the tradesmen who remained had sent away their families: so that in less than six days from the commencement of the outbreak, the most afflicted streets were deserted by more than three-quarters of their inhabitants.

There were a few cases of cholera in the neighborhood of Broad Street, Golden Square, in the latter part of August; and the so-called outbreak, which commenced in the night between the 31st August and the 1st September, was, as in all similar instances, only a violent increase of the malady. As soon as I became acquainted with the situation and extent of this irruption of cholera, I suspected some contamination of the water of the much-frequented street-pump in Broad Street, near the end of Cambridge Street; but on examining the water, on the evening of the 3rd September, I found so little impurity in it of an organic nature, that I hesitated to come to a conclusion. Further inquiry, however, showed me that there was no other circumstance or agent common to the circumscribed locality in which this sudden increase of cholera occurred, and not extending beyond it, except the water of the above mentioned pump. I found, moreover, that the water varied, during the next two days, in the amount of organic impurity, visible to the naked eye, on close inspection, in the form of small white, flocculent particles; and I concluded that, at the commencement of the outbreak, it might possibly have been still more impure. I requested permission, therefore, to take a list, at the General Register Office, of the deaths from cholera, registered during the week ending 2nd September, in the subdistricts of Golden Square, Berwick Street, and St. Ann's, Soho, which was kindly granted. Eighty-nine deaths from cholera were registered, during the week, in the three subdistricts. Of these, only six occurred in the four first days of the week; four occurred on Thursday, the 31st August; and the remaining seventy-nine on Friday and Saturday. I considered, therefore, that the outbreak

(Continued)

Figure 4.7 (Continued)

commenced on the Thursday; and I made inquiry, in detail, respecting the eighty-three deaths registered as having taken place during the last three days of the week.

On proceeding to the spot, I found that nearly all the deaths had taken place within a short distance of the pump. There were only ten deaths in houses situated decidedly nearer to another street pump. In five of these cases the families of the deceased persons informed me that they always sent to the pump in Broad Street, as they preferred the water to that of the pump which was nearer. In three other cases, the deceased were children who went to school near the pump in Broad Street. Two of them were known to drink the water; and the parents of the third think it probable that it did so. The other two deaths, beyond the district which this pump supplies, represent only the amount of mortality from cholera that was occurring before the irruption took place.

With regard to the deaths occurring in the locality belonging to the pump, there were sixty-one instances in which I was informed that the deceased persons used to drink the pump-water from Broad Street, either constantly, or occasionally. In six instances I could get no information, owing to the death or departure of everyone connected with the deceased individuals; and in six cases I was informed that the deceased persons did not drink the pump-water before their illness.

The result of the inquiry then was, that there had been no particular outbreak or increase of cholera, in this part of London, except among the persons who were in the habit of drinking the water of the above-mentioned pump-well.

I had an interview with the Board of Guardians of St. James's parish, on the evening of Thursday, 7th September, and represented the above circumstances to them. In consequence of what I said, the handle of the pump was removed on the following day.

Table 1   Grid Location of Deaths Due to Cholera in 1854 London, Plus Water Pumps and Brewery Locations

Water Pump Locations	Brewery Location	#	Deaths Due to Cholera—Grid Locations									
			Day 1	Day 2	Day 3	Day 4	Day 5	Day 6	Day 7	Day 8	Day 9	Day 10
		1	L18	S4	G6	J15	G6	S14	P6	G6	Q15	M8
		2	R14	P13	R11	O11	T10	W14	Q14	O11	W10	R11
T6	X13	3	O15	O9	T14	O14	P14	K15	O16	N16	N6	R11
D7	X14	4	M13	N16	P11	O13	T10	R11	N13	R15	J11	M15
P7	X15	5	O11	L9	R14	T14	M8	Q15	J15	N9	M9	O15
G11	Y13	6	L17	Q16	M16	U17	N16	J16	O17	J19	X19	M17
P14	Y14	7	N16	S13	Q12	T18	P17	P11	M17	N17	U12	S15
Y14	Y15	8	M14	O12	L13	N11	N14	R15	O14	N13	S19	U14
I16		9	R13	S14	O12	N14	N14	M11	P16	N16	R15	S13
Z18		10	N14	Q15	P13	O12	M11	M11	L17	L17	L18	J16
J20		11	O16	O22	O9	T9	M8	G22	T9	T9	M9	L11
D21		12	N12	Q14	Q13	N17	K17	S13	L11	O15	N13	X19
L26		13	N12	N14	N14	M14	R15	Q12	N13	N15	R16	M15
		14	U20	O15	M12	P15	M14	Q15	S12	J15	S12	L17
		15	O14	O8	M17	P8	P8	M8	P6	P9	Q20	U20
		16	Q15	P17	J19	M15	N14	R11	P11	Q15	O13	L18
		17	P8	O18	L17	R16	P16	M13	N14	P15	P12	O22
		18	T9	R16	R14	M13	S15	K15	M16	Q12	R20	L21
		19	O13	T15	O14	K12	K12	P17	K15	R16	O5	O15
		20	O23	Q13	K15	P8	R14	R15	O12	Q16	J15	U20

(Continued)

Table 1 (Continued)

Water Pump Locations	Brewery Location	#	Day 1	Day 2	Day 3	Day 4	Day 5	Day 6	Day 7	Day 8	Day 9	Day 10
							Deaths Due to Cholera—Grid Locations					
		21	R15	J12	R15	M17	R14	R13	O12	U14	U14	O16
		22	N17	L13	N16	N12	N13	N17	P9	N9	L17	O16
		23	P11	K20	N14	N14	N12	R14	G19	U20	K14	L11
		24	M14	P11	M14	N17	Q15	H19	N15	N12	P23	K17
		25	P13	U20	M14	J16	W17	Q16	K14	K14	L18	R20
		26	L18	O17	L13	L17	M15	Q20	N16	N12	M15	S19
		27	M11	Q15	N14	Q15	N13	G6	R15	M17	L18	O8
		28	N13	N16	Q17	L13	M17	M11	J11	Q15	M8	M11
		29	L13	S19	N8	M13	Q16	P15	L8	P9	F17	M13
		30	R8	U6	Q15	N16	L13	R16	R14	T21	U20	
		31	P14	T21	L18	L9	M8	R15	R11	N11	L18	
		32		M13	R20	O8	P6	L8	T13	L9	T13	
		33		N13	L18	T21	N23	P9	P11	M11		
		34		N13	P6	N9	P13	P11	K9	U20		
		35		N13	S12	N13	M11	O13	N13			
		36		P14	P13	N11	M12	O13	N16			
		37			L9	L11	O13	P14	T21			
		38			O13	O21						
		39				G23						
		40				S14						
		Total	31	36	38	40	37	37	37	34	31	29

Exhibit 1   Map Showing the Location of Deaths From Cholera in Soho District of London and Location of Water Pump Sites

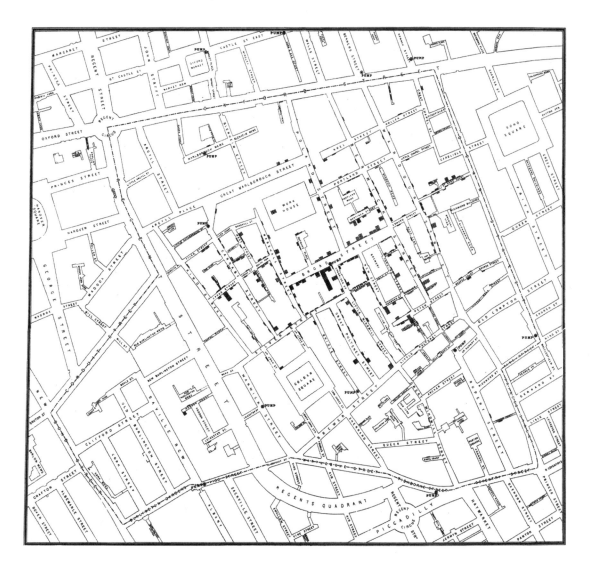

Source: Excerpt from *On the Mode of Communication of Cholera* by John Snow, MD. London: John Churchill, New Burlington Street, England, 1855 (pp. 38–55).

Available for download from **www.corwin.com/textdependentquestions**

Videos

To read a QR code, you must have a smartphone or tablet with a camera. We recommend that you download a QR code reader app that is made specifically for your phone or tablet brand.

Videos can also be accessed at
www.corwin.com/textdependentquestions

Video 4.1 Students in Lisa Forehand's kindergarten class discuss textual evidence to determine why the characters in *The Day the Crayons Quit* acted as they did.

Video 4.2 Alex Cabrera introduces his second grade class to a new example of supply and demand to relate to the text they previously read about cow farmers' milk prices.

Video 4.3 Students in Shawna Codrington's second grade class talk about the moral of *Lon Po Po* based on their annotations before comparing it to *Little Red Riding Hood*.

Video 4.4 Melissa Noble's fourth grade students share their opinions about character traits and textual themes by comparing two folktales.

5

WHAT DOES THE TEXT *INSPIRE YOU TO DO*?

In building the habit of reading closely, teachers are less like the sage on the stage and more like the guide on the side. A trail guide, if you will. Like a trail guide, teachers have specialized knowledge of the terrain, and they can point out interesting sights and warn of pitfalls. But trail guides understand that the experience any one traveler has on the journey will be a shade different from the experience of all the other travelers. A trail guide hopes that the journey itself will influence each person in some way. Like a good trail guide, a skilled teacher shows you where to look but doesn't tell you what to think.

The journey through a complex print, digital, or multimedia text requires a guide to shepherd children through an unfamiliar landscape—someone who hones the novices' observational powers in order to deepen their understanding of what they are witnessing. This then cultivates within them the habit of reading closely, and it is something they will continue to develop and refine over their lifetimes. In classrooms, teachers show students a path for journeying through the text, pointing out the interesting details and providing space for them to coconstruct an understanding of what the text offers. This, again, is close reading—an instructional routine. The previous chapters have been devoted to developing the habit of reading closely in order to determine

- *What the text says* through *inspection* (the literal interpretation)

- *How the text works* through *investigation* (the structural interpretation)

- *What the text means* through *interpretation* (the inferential interpretation)

This process is not strictly linear. Engaged readers roam across the landscape of a text with little regard for the teacher's lesson plan. Carefully prepared sequences of questions are discarded in situations where students find themselves naturally discussing, in advance, the very concepts that subsequent questions would have asked them to address (something that occurs more frequently as students become more skilled at reading closely). Even still, the text-dependent questions prepared for a series of discussions about a compelling text serve the important purpose of setting some trail markers for the guide and the travelers to follow. And eventually a good trail should lead somewhere.

When it comes to text, the destination is a product of some kind. Perhaps it is a debate, or a Socratic seminar. Maybe it's a presentation or a piece of writing. The destination might lie in taking action to write a letter to a government representative or to develop a fundraising activity. It may come in the form of a shared investigation—a call for students to seek out more information about a topic or to write a report. There are a host of possible destinations, but they have one thing in common: They change the reader in some way. The reader comes to know more about a topic, to be intrigued by a new idea, or to be troubled by an injustice he or she hadn't known existed. The text may illuminate corners of students they hadn't noticed before, or cause them to consider another person's dilemmas differently, or built a sense of affiliation with others. In other words, it becomes a part of who they are as thinkers and as people. So our final cognitive path sets them, and us, off to explore the question, *what does the text inspire you, the reader, to do?*

An Invitation to Read Closely:
Action-Oriented Questions and Tasks

All writers hope to transform the thinking of their readers. Texts may confirm what you, the reader, already suspected about an idea but needed to have validated. Or they might cause you to question, critique, or take action. In every case, the text is integrated into readers' knowledge of themselves and their world. But integration doesn't come in advance of action—it happens as a result of action. How often have you caught yourself noticing what you thought while in the act of explaining your thoughts to someone else? You realize you didn't know what you thought about something until you said it. We spur students to take action precisely because it gives them the opportunity to consolidate and clarify.

Taking action doesn't mean being militant. It's not that every reading lends itself to social change. In fact, many of the texts we teach in school are not for that purpose at all. Taking action means applying what has been learned by creating something new. And in the act of creating something new, learners build a sense of autonomy. In this way, students learn to take responsibility for their own learning, and manage their time and resources. Students figure out how to prioritize tasks and calibrate their work with others (Fisher & Frey, 2014a).

> The text-dependent questions prepared for a series of discussions about a compelling text serve the important purpose of setting some trail markers for the guide and the travelers to follow.

Why Students Need to Complete These Types of Tasks

Learning advances when students are able to transform information into products. The notion of the student as a blank slate has long since been disproven, and we have a far better understanding of the value of active learning (Marzano, Pickering, & Heflebower, 2011). Experiential learning and problem-based learning, to name two theoretical orientations, utilize this element of learning extensively to drive instruction. But other learning models also can be used to help students understand *what the text means* at a deeper level and to figure out what the text inspires them to do. For example, critical literacy theory is predicated on an assumption that students examine information with an eye toward action. They examine power structures, seek out alternative perspectives, and formulate problems (McLaughlin & DeVoogd, 2004). In each of these theoretical models, the intent is for learners to transform knowledge into something that is meaningful and integrated into their worldview. At its best, action should adequately answer the question every student has, namely, "Why do I need to learn this?"

Knowledge formation moves from initial acquisition to transfer of knowledge in novel situations. In the groundbreaking work, *How People Learn: Brain, Mind, Experience, and School* (Bransford, Brown, & Cocking, 2000) the principles of transfer are summarized as follows:

- Knowledge that is overly contextualized can reduce transfer; abstract representations of knowledge can help promote transfer.

- Transfer is best viewed as an active, dynamic process rather than a passive end-product of a particular set of learning experiences.

- All new learning involves transfer based on previous learning, and this fact has important implications for the design of instruction that helps students learn. (p. 53)

Each of these points is worthy of further discussion, with the first sounding a cautionary bell. The evidence suggests that when students learn how to apply a skill only within a very specific context or in a single, narrowly defined space, they are less likely to apply it in a novel situation. For example, children who are tasked with rote memorization of an isolated list of vocabulary terms are unlikely to understand those words or phrases when encountered in texts. On the other hand, tasks that require students to utilize new information across a broader platform are more likely to activate their knowledge more effectively and accurately. That's why effective vocabulary instruction includes textual experiences ripe with opportunities for students to resolve unknown vocabulary using structural analysis, context clues, and resources (Frey & Fisher, 2009).

Transfer relies on a dynamic process "that requires learners to actively choose and evaluate strategies, consider resources, and receive feedback" (Bransford, Brown, & Cocking, 2000, p. 66). Learners need the space, opportunity, and time to interact with texts, concepts, and one another in order not only to create products that reflect their knowledge of the content presented, but also to demonstrate

> Learning advances when students are able to transform information into products.

how they have transformed that knowledge by making it their own. Examples of these dynamic processes include

- Continued interactions with the teacher through conferring

- Productive small group work with peers

- Investigation and research

- Writing

- Other meaningful formative and summative assessment practices

Previous learning plays an essential role in the transfer of knowledge, and all learners can and should apply their background knowledge and prior experiences judiciously in the creation of new knowledge. The caution about the role of personal meaning-making in close reading practices has been a point of contention among scholars and practitioners. We have heard caring educators express concern about their abilities to engage and motivate students in the absence of discussion about personal connections. Likewise, we have heard equally caring educators express their concerns about privileging the personal experiences of some students at the expense of others. We believe that both camps make important points. Previous learning, both in and out of school, is an essential element in the process of transfer, as it is the means we all use to deepen new knowledge. At the same time, we must be more aware that tasks that move students too far away from the texts at hand create an unequal playing field, with some able to draw on a deeper well of personal experiences that others do not possess.

Therefore, task design is essential, and it should strike a balance between utilizing the information gleaned from the text and accompanying discussions, on the one hand, and providing a further opportunity to create new knowledge on the other. This is a point at which students can meet levels 3 and 4 of the Depth of Knowledge task demands (Webb, 2002). In this phase of learning, students analyze arguments to note what is missing or incomplete, or what warrants further investigation. They construct their own arguments using logic and reasoning, and they formulate a plan of action for

> Learners need the space, opportunity, and time to interact with texts, concepts, and one another in order not only to create products that reflect their knowledge of the content presented, but also to demonstrate how they have transformed that knowledge by making it their own.

next steps in their learning. The learning happens over an extended period of time, especially in terms of the preparation needed to write a report, design a presentation, complete a shared investigation, or compile information for use in a debate. Importantly, completion of these tasks does not automatically serve as evidence of a greater depth of knowledge. For instance, a presentation could just as easily entail the replication and recall of knowledge. For that reason, the construction of the task is vital.

Natalia Sherbinsky's fourth grade students read and discussed *Riding Freedom* (Ryan, 1999) over two weeks. Close reading lessons were interspersed with independent reading outside of school and peer-led inquiry circles in the classroom (Daniels & Harvey, 2009).

During their small group work meetings throughout the unit, students annotated text, developed their notebooks, and, at the conclusion, formulated a question for inquiry. One group decided to engage in a mini-inquiry about Charlie (Charlotte) Parkhurst, the real-life

Students engage in a lively group discussion.

stagecoach driver on whom the novel is based. Another group decided to interview the local mounted police officer in charge of the horse stable for their city's police department. Meanwhile, a third group of students determined that they would investigate other women who played important roles in the California Gold Rush. A fourth group wanted to follow up on the author's life and works, since several had read other stories written by her. Ms. Sherbinsky had her students use the search engine called SweetSearch, which contains websites that have been vetted by other educators, to locate additional information about their topics. The students spent two days compiling the research needed for their mini-inquiry and a third day developing a final product for a gallery walk.

On the fourth day, groups shared their findings and were able to explore the findings of their peers. These short informal listening sessions, conducted as part of the gallery walk, featured a poster of the project, narration about the inquiry question, and a QR code so that students could listen to the narration on their tablets. [These were created using the Audioboo app https://itunes.apple.com/us/app/audioboo/id305204540?mt=8]. The first group wrote a short FAQ (frequently asked questions) document about Parkhurst. The second group recorded and edited a short video capture of their interview with the mounted police officer about the care of working horses. The third group made a poster about three women from the Gold Rush era. The fourth group gathered information from the publisher's website and the author's own. Ms. Sherbinsky was pleased with the outcomes and their use of technology to create their final projects.

"I'm learning that I don't need to devote as much time as I did in the past to these inquiries," said the teacher. "I used to get so caught up in the arts and crafts side of it, and that's what really eats up the time. This is about inquiry, not how much glitter you use on a poster." Noting that the posters had simple visuals and a QR code, she offered, "They're understanding that the content is what's important. They know they've only got three minutes of narration time at their disposal, so they are learning to make it count." About the short time line, she simply laughed and said, "It's amazing how much they get done when there's a sense of urgency! They knew the listening gallery would be held Thursday morning, which made getting down to work so much more important when they started on Monday."

> Previous learning, both in and out of school, is an essential element in the process of transfer, as it is the means we all use to deepen new knowledge.

Students practice interviewing each other on a mobile device.

How Examining *What the Text Inspires You to Do* Addresses the STANDARDS

Reading Standards

The targeted standards in this group fall squarely under the cluster of integration of knowledge and ideas. As discussed in the previous chapter, **standards 7** and **9** speak to the need to contextualize readings across authors, media platforms, themes, and perspectives. **Standard 8** calls for a more specialized text that provides a springboard for examining the role of reasoning and evidence. Not all texts do so; you'll notice that this standard is not listed with literary texts, but only with informational ones. A table displaying the reading standards that focus on how texts inspire action can be found in Figure 5.1.

Figure 5.1 ELA Reading Standards That Focus on *What the Text Inspires You to Do*

Standard (Grade)	Literary	Informational
7 (K)	With prompting and support, describe the relationship between illustrations and the story in which they appear (e.g., what moment in a story an illustration depicts).	With prompting and support, describe the relationship between illustrations and the text in which they appear (e.g., what person, place, thing, or idea in the text an illustration depicts).
7 (1)	Use illustrations and details in a story to describe its characters, setting, or events.	Use the illustrations and details in a text to describe its key ideas.
7 (2)	Use information gained from the illustrations and words in a print or digital text to demonstrate understanding of its characters, setting, or plot.	Explain how specific images (e.g., a diagram showing how a machine works) contribute to and clarify a text.
7 (3)	Explain how specific aspects of a text's illustrations contribute to what is conveyed by the words in a story (e.g., create mood, emphasize aspects of a character or setting).	Use information gained from illustrations (e.g., maps, photographs) and the words in a text to demonstrate understanding of the text (e.g., where, when, why, and how key events occur).
7 (4)	Make connections between the text of a story or drama and a visual or oral presentation of the text, identifying where each version reflects specific descriptions and directions in the text.	Interpret information presented visually, orally, or quantitatively (e.g., in charts, graphs, diagrams, time lines, animations, or interactive elements on Web pages) and explain how the information contributes to an understanding of the text in which it appears.
7 (5)	Analyze how visual and multimedia elements contribute to the meaning, tone, or beauty of a text (e.g., graphic novel, multimedia presentation of fiction, folktale, myth, poem).	Draw on information from multiple print or digital sources, demonstrating the ability to locate an answer to a question quickly or to solve a problem efficiently.

Standard (Grade)	Literary	Informational
8 (K)	(Not applicable to literature)	With prompting and support, identify the reasons an author gives to support points in a text.
8 (1)	(Not applicable to literature)	Identify the reasons an author gives to support points in a text.
8 (2)	(Not applicable to literature)	Describe how reasons support specific points the author makes in a text.
8 (3)	(Not applicable to literature)	Describe the logical connection between particular sentences and paragraphs in a text (e.g., comparison, cause/effect, first/second/third in a sequence).
8 (4)	(Not applicable to literature)	Explain how an author uses reasons and evidence to support particular points in a text.
8 (5)	(Not applicable to literature)	Explain how an author uses reasons and evidence to support particular points in a text, identifying which reasons and evidence support which point(s).
9 (K)	With prompting and support, compare and contrast the adventures and experiences of characters in familiar stories.	With prompting and support, identify basic similarities in and differences between two texts on the same topic (e.g., in illustrations, descriptions, or procedures).
9 (1)	Compare and contrast the adventures and experiences of characters in stories.	Identify basic similarities in and differences between two texts on the same topic (e.g., in illustrations, descriptions, or procedures).
9 (2)	Compare and contrast two or more versions of the same story (e.g., Cinderella stories) by different authors or from different cultures.	Compare and contrast the most important points presented by two texts on the same topic.
9 (3)	Compare and contrast the themes, settings, and plots of stories written by the same author about the same or similar characters (e.g., in books from a series).	Compare and contrast the most important points and key details presented in two texts on the same topic.
9 (4)	Compare and contrast the treatment of similar themes and topics (e.g., opposition of good and evil) and patterns of events (e.g., the quest) in stories, myths, and traditional literature from different cultures.	Integrate information from two texts on the same topic in order to write or speak about the subject knowledgeably.
9 (5)	Compare and contrast stories in the same genre (e.g., mysteries and adventure stories) on their approaches to similar themes and topics.	Integrate information from several texts on the same topic in order to write or speak about the subject knowledgeably.

(Continued)

Figure 5.1   (Continued)

Standard (Grade)	Literary	Informational
10 (K)	Actively engage in group reading activities with purpose and understanding.	
10 (1)	With prompting and support, read prose and poetry of appropriate complexity for grade 1.	With prompting and support, read informational texts appropriately complex for grade 1.
10 (2)	By the end of the year, read and comprehend literature, including stories and poetry, in the grades 2–3 text complexity band proficiently, with scaffolding as needed at the high end of the range.	By the end of year, read and comprehend informational texts, including history/social studies, science, and technical texts, in the grades 2–3 text complexity band proficiently, with scaffolding as needed at the high end of the range.
10 (3)	By the end of the year, read and comprehend literature, including stories, dramas, and poetry, at the high end of the grades 2–3 text complexity band independently and proficiently.	By the end of the year, read and comprehend informational texts, including history/social studies, science, and technical texts, at the high end of the grades 2–3 text complexity band independently and proficiently.
10 (4)	By the end of the year, read and comprehend literature, including stories, dramas, and poetry, in the grades 4–5 text complexity band proficiently, with scaffolding as needed at the high end of the range.	By the end of year, read and comprehend informational texts, including history/social studies, science, and technical texts, in the grades 4–5 text complexity band proficiently, with scaffolding as needed at the high end of the range.
10 (5)	By the end of the year, read and comprehend literature, including stories, dramas, and poetry, at the high end of the grades 4–5 text complexity band independently and proficiently.	By the end of the year, read and comprehend informational texts, including history/social studies, science, and technical texts, at the high end of the grades 4–5 text complexity band independently and proficiently.

Language Standards

The language standards regarding conventions in speaking and writing continue in importance as students respond to tasks that ask them to create products (see Figure 5.2). **Standard 3** is worth noting in this context, because with this standard, the issues of language function and style take center stage. Each of the tasks profiled in this chapter (presentation, debate, writing, Socratic seminar, shared investigation, and research) demands an understanding of these issues. While some of these tasks may require students to utilize face-to-face interaction, others may use the printed word as the platform. These take on a further dimension as students must consider whether the function is to explain and inform, persuade, or convey an experience. Finally, the composition of the audience must be considered. Working on extemporaneous and prepared speeches, presentations, and debates, as well as on more formal writing provides students with

Figure 5.2 Language Standards That Focus on *What the Text Inspires You to Do*

	Kindergarten	Grade 1	Grade 2	Grade 3	Grade 4	Grade 5
1	Demonstrate command of the conventions of standard English grammar and usage when writing or speaking.	Demonstrate command of the conventions of standard English grammar and usage when writing or speaking.	Demonstrate command of the conventions of standard English grammar and usage when writing or speaking.	Demonstrate command of the conventions of standard English grammar and usage when writing or speaking.	Demonstrate command of the conventions of standard English grammar and usage when writing or speaking.	Demonstrate command of the conventions of standard English grammar and usage when writing or speaking.
	a. Print many upper- and lowercase letters.	a. Print all upper- and lowercase letters.	a. Use collective nouns (e.g., *group*).	a. Explain the function of nouns, pronouns, verbs, adjectives, and adverbs in general and their functions in particular sentences.	a. Use relative pronouns (*who, whose, whom, which, that*) and relative adverbs (*where, when, why*).	a. Explain the function of conjunctions, prepositions, and interjections in general and their function in particular sentences.
	b. Use frequently occurring nouns and verbs.	b. Use common, proper, and possessive nouns.	b. Form and use frequently occurring irregular plural nouns (e.g., *feet, children, teeth, mice, fish*).	b. Form and use regular and irregular plural nouns.	b. Form and use the progressive (e.g., *I was walking; I am walking; I will be walking*) verb tenses.	b. Form and use the perfect (e.g., *I had walked; I have walked; I will have walked*) verb tenses.
	c. Form regular plural nouns orally by adding /s/ or /es/ (e.g., *dog, dogs; wish, wishes*).	c. Use singular and plural nouns with matching verbs in basic sentences (e.g., *He hops; We hop*).	c. Use reflexive pronouns (e.g., *myself, ourselves*).	c. Use abstract nouns (e.g., *childhood*).	c. Use modal auxiliaries (e.g., *can, may, must*) to convey various conditions.	c. Use verb tense to convey various times, sequences, states, and conditions.
	d. Understand and use question words (interrogatives) (e.g., *who, what, where, when, why, how*).	d. Use personal, possessive, and indefinite pronouns (e.g., *I, me, my; they, them, their; anyone, everything*).	d. Form and use the past tense of frequently occurring irregular verbs (e.g., *sat, hid, told*).	d. Form and use regular and irregular verbs.	d. Order adjectives within sentences according to conventional patterns (e.g., *a small red bag* rather than *a red small bag*).	d. Recognize and correct inappropriate shifts in verb tense.
	e. Use the most frequently occurring prepositions (e.g., *to, from, in, out, on, off, for, of, by, with*).	e. Use verbs to convey a sense of past, present, and future (e.g., *Yesterday I walked home; Today I walk home; Tomorrow I will walk home*).	e. Use adjectives and adverbs, and choose between them depending on what is to be modified.	e. Form and use the simple (e.g., *I walked; I walk; I will walk*) verb tenses.		e. Use correlative conjunctions (e.g., *either/or, neither/nor*).
				f. Ensure subject-verb and pronoun-antecedent agreement.		

(Continued)

Figure 5.2 (Continued)

Kindergarten	Grade 1	Grade 2	Grade 3	Grade 4	Grade 5
f. Produce and expand complete sentences in shared language activities.	f. Use frequently occurring adjectives. g. Use frequently occurring conjunctions (e.g., and, but, or, so, because). h. Use determiners (e.g., articles, demonstratives). i. Use frequently occurring prepositions (e.g., during, beyond, toward). j. Produce and expand complete simple and compound declarative, interrogative, imperative, and exclamatory sentences in response to prompts.	f. Produce, expand, and rearrange complete simple and compound sentences (e.g., The boy watched the movie; The little boy watched the movie; The action movie was watched by the little boy).	g. Form and use comparative and superlative adjectives and adverbs, and choose between them depending on what is to be modified. h. Use coordinating and subordinating conjunctions. i. Produce simple, compound, and complex sentences.	e. Form and use prepositional phrases. f. Produce complete sentences, recognizing and correcting inappropriate fragments and run-ons. g. Correctly use frequently confused words (e.g., to, too, two; there, their).	
Demonstrate command of the conventions of standard English capitalization, punctuation, and spelling when writing.	Demonstrate command of the conventions of standard English capitalization, punctuation, and spelling when writing.	Demonstrate command of the conventions of standard English capitalization, punctuation, and spelling when writing.	Demonstrate command of the conventions of standard English capitalization, punctuation, and spelling when writing.	Demonstrate command of the conventions of standard English capitalization, punctuation, and spelling when writing.	Demonstrate command of the conventions of standard English capitalization, punctuation, and spelling when writing.

2 | Demonstrate command of the conventions of standard English capitalization, punctuation, and spelling when writing.

Kindergarten	Grade 1	Grade 2	Grade 3	Grade 4	Grade 5
a. Capitalize the first word in a sentence and the pronoun *I*.	a. Capitalize dates and names of people.	a. Capitalize holidays, product names, and geographic names.	a. Capitalize appropriate words in titles.	a. Use correct capitalization.	a. Use punctuation to separate items in a series.
b. Recognize and name end punctuation.	b. Use end punctuation for sentences.	b. Use commas in greetings and closings of letters.	b. Use commas in addresses.	b. Use commas and quotation marks to mark direct speech and quotations from a text.	b. Use a comma to separate an introductory element from the rest of the sentence.
c. Write a letter or letters for most consonant and short-vowel sounds (phonemes).	c. Use commas in dates and to separate single words in a series.	c. Use an apostrophe to form contractions and frequently occurring possessives.	c. Use commas and quotation marks in dialogue.	c. Use a comma before a coordinating conjunction in a compound sentence.	c. Use a comma to set off the words yes and no (e.g., *Yes, thank you*), to set off a tag question from the rest of the sentence (e.g., *It's true, isn't it?*), and to indicate direct address (e.g., *Is that you, Steve?*).
d. Spell simple words phonetically, drawing on knowledge of sound-letter relationships.	d. Use conventional spelling for words with common spelling patterns and for frequently occurring irregular words.	d. Generalize learned spelling patterns when writing words (e.g., cage → badge; boy → boil).	d. Form and use possessives.	d. Spell grade-appropriate words correctly, consulting references as needed.	d. Use underlining, quotation marks, or italics to indicate titles of works.
	e. Spell untaught words phonetically, drawing on phonemic awareness and spelling conventions.	e. Consult reference materials, including beginning dictionaries, as needed to check and correct spellings.	e. Use conventional spelling for high-frequency and other studied words and for adding suffixes to base words (e.g., *sitting, smiled, cries, happiness*).		e. Spell grade-appropriate words correctly, consulting references as needed.
			f. Use spelling patterns and generalizations (e.g., word families, position-based spellings, syllable patterns, ending rules, meaningful word parts) in writing words.		
			g. Consult reference materials, including beginning dictionaries, as needed to check and correct spellings.		

(Continued)

Figure 5.2 (Continued)

	Kindergarten	Grade 1	Grade 2	Grade 3	Grade 4	Grade 5
3	(Begins in grade 2)	(Begins in grade 2)	Use knowledge of language and its conventions when writing, speaking, reading, or listening. a. Compare formal and informal uses of English.	Use knowledge of language and its conventions when writing, speaking, reading, or listening. a. Choose words and phrases for effect. b. Recognize and observe differences between the conventions of spoken and written standard English.	Use knowledge of language and its conventions when writing, speaking, reading, or listening. a. Choose words and phrases to convey ideas precisely. b. Choose punctuation for effect. c. Differentiate between contexts that call for formal English (e.g., presenting ideas) and situations where informal discourse is appropriate (e.g., small-group discussion).	Use knowledge of language and its conventions when writing, speaking, reading, or listening. a. Expand, combine, and reduce sentences for meaning, reader/listener interest, and style. b. Compare and contrast the varieties of English (e.g., dialects, registers) used in stories, dramas, or poems.
6	Use words and phrases acquired through conversations, reading and being read to, and responding to texts.	Use words and phrases acquired through conversations, reading and being read to, and responding to texts, including using frequently occurring conjunctions to signal simple relationships (e.g., because).	Use words and phrases acquired through conversations, reading and being read to, and responding to texts, including using adjectives and adverbs to describe (e.g., When other kids are happy that makes me happy).	Acquire and use accurately grade-appropriate conversational, general academic, and domain specific words and phrases, including those that signal spatial and temporal relationships (e.g., After dinner that night we went looking for them).	Acquire and use accurately grade-appropriate general academic and domain-specific words and phrases, including those that signal precise actions, emotions, or states of being (e.g., quizzed, whined, stammered) and that are basic to a particular topic (e.g., wildlife, conservation, and endangered when discussing animal preservation).	Acquire and use accurately grade-appropriate general academic and domain-specific words and phrases, including those that signal contrast, addition, and other logical relationships (e.g., however, although, nevertheless, similarly, moreover, in addition).

opportunities to consider audience as a key factor in their design. Students must ask themselves, *Is my audience my fellow classmates, or someone who doesn't know me?*

The first grade students in Henry Lee's science class take photographs each day of the progress their seeds are making. Using their classroom tablets, pairs of students take a digital photograph and then meet to discuss how the plant has changed since the previous day. The photographs are compiled into a simple stop-action video clip so that students can compare each day's growth with growth on all the previous days. "After they have met with their partners to discuss it, they compose a simple statement about the status of the plant in their digital journals," said Mr. Lee. "By the time the plant has grown for a few weeks, they have both a visual and written record of its growth. We can then talk about our data and compare results. And in the meantime, I have a useful product to view, which really helps me gauge their progress in the science content. Plus, the kids like to watch each other's movies!" he said.

Speaking and Listening Standards

The speaking and listening standards, essential throughout text-based discussion, remain on center stage at this phase of instruction (see Figure 5.3). **Standard 5** in speaking and listening appears for the first time, as it addresses the need for students to make presentations that include multimedia and visual displays of information. This standard acknowledges the growing importance of visual literacy in contemporary life (e.g., Eisner, 1991). Each of the other tasks draws, to a lesser or more significant degree, on the remaining speaking and listening standards.

For example, third grade students in Jayla Lewis's class record themselves reciting the Claude McKay poem "After the Winter" and select five digital photographs that they believe represent the images in the poem. "I put all of them on a loop and play them during our spring Back to School night," she said. "The families and the students love hearing their own children in a recitation and admire the pictures the children have selected," she said. "This project has really grown," said Ms. Lewis. "What initially began as a fun activity of getting to see familiar people recite a poem has turned into something more. Next year I'm going to expand the number of poems we use."

Writing Standards

Because this phase of instruction is action-based, writing makes its first appearance in this chapter. We know that spontaneous writing, annotation, and note taking occur through the previous phases, but we chose to spotlight these standards more formally here because most of them speak to the qualities of finished products. **Standards 1–3** concern themselves with text types, specifically those constructed to

1. Present opinion with evidence

2. Explain or inform

3. Convey real and imagined experiences

Figure 5.3 Speaking and Listening Standards That Focus on *What the Text Inspires You to Do*

	Kindergarten	Grade 1	Grade 2	Grade 3	Grade 4	Grade 5
1	Participate in collaborative conversations with diverse partners about *kindergarten topics and texts* with peers and adults in small and larger groups. a. Follow agreed-upon rules for discussions (e.g., listening to others and taking turns speaking about the topics and texts under discussion). b. Continue a conversation through multiple exchanges.	Participate in collaborative conversations with diverse partners about *grade 1 topics and texts* with peers and adults in small and larger groups. a. Follow agreed-upon rules for discussions (e.g., listening to others with care, speaking one at a time about the topics and texts under discussion). b. Build on others' talk in conversations by responding to the comments of others through multiple exchanges. c. Ask questions to clear up any confusion about the topics and texts under discussion.	Participate in collaborative conversations with diverse partners about *grade 2 topics and texts* with peers and adults in small and larger groups. a. Follow agreed-upon rules for discussions (e.g., gaining the floor in respectful ways, listening to others with care, speaking one at a time about the topics and texts under discussion). b. Build on others' talk in conversations by linking their comments to the remarks of others. c. Ask for clarification and further explanation as needed about the topics and texts under discussion.	Engage effectively in a range of collaborative discussions (one-on-one, in groups, and teacher-led) with diverse partners on *grade 3 topics and texts*, building on others' ideas and expressing their own clearly. a. Come to discussions prepared, having read or studied required material; explicitly draw on that preparation and other information known about the topic to explore ideas under discussion. b. Follow agreed-upon rules for discussions (e.g., gaining the floor in respectful ways, listening to others with care, speaking one at a time about the topics and texts under discussion).	Engage effectively in a range of collaborative discussions (one-on-one, in groups, and teacher-led) with diverse partners on *grade 4 topics and texts*, building on others' ideas and expressing their own clearly. a. Come to discussions prepared, having read or studied required material; explicitly draw on that preparation and other information known about the topic to explore ideas under discussion. b. Follow agreed-upon rules for discussions and carry out assigned roles. c. Pose and respond to specific questions to clarify or follow up on information, and	Engage effectively in a range of collaborative discussions (one-on-one, in groups, and teacher-led) with diverse partners on *grade 5 topics and texts*, building on others' ideas and expressing their own clearly. a. Come to discussions prepared, having read or studied required material; explicitly draw on that preparation and other information known about the topic to explore ideas under discussion. b. Follow agreed-upon rules for discussions and carry out assigned roles. c. Pose and respond to specific questions by making comments that contribute to

Kindergarten	Grade 1	Grade 2	Grade 3	Grade 4	Grade 5
			c. Ask questions to check understanding of information presented, stay on topic, and link their comments to the remarks of others. d. Explain their own ideas and understanding in light of the discussion.	make comments that contribute to the discussion and link to the remarks of others. d. Review the key ideas expressed and explain their own ideas and understanding in light of the discussion.	the discussion and elaborate on the remarks of others. d. Review the key ideas expressed and draw conclusions in light of information and knowledge gained from the discussions.
2 Confirm understanding of a text read aloud or information presented orally or through other media by asking and answering questions about key details and requesting clarification if something is not understood.	Ask and answer questions about key details in a text read aloud or information presented orally or through other media.	Recount or describe key ideas or details from a text read aloud or information presented orally or through other media.	Determine the main ideas and supporting details of a text read aloud or information presented in diverse media and formats, including visually, quantitatively, and orally.	Paraphrase portions of a text read aloud or information presented in diverse media and formats, including visually, quantitatively, and orally.	Summarize a written text read aloud or information presented in diverse media and formats, including visually, quantitatively, and orally.
3 Ask and answer questions in order to seek help, get information, or clarify something that is not understood.	Ask and answer questions about what a speaker says in order to gather additional information or clarify something that is not understood.	Ask and answer questions about what a speaker says in order to clarify comprehension, gather additional information, or deepen understanding of a topic or issue.	Ask and answer questions about information from a speaker, offering appropriate elaboration and detail.	Identify the reasons and evidence a speaker provides to support particular points.	Summarize the points a speaker makes and explain how each claim is supported by reasons and evidence.

(Continued)

Figure 5.3 (Continued)

	Kindergarten	Grade 1	Grade 2	Grade 3	Grade 4	Grade 5
4	Describe familiar people, places, things, and events and, with prompting and support, provide additional detail.	Describe people, places, things, and events with relevant details, expressing ideas and feelings clearly.	Tell a story or recount an experience with appropriate facts and relevant, descriptive details, speaking audibly in coherent sentences.	Report on a topic or text, tell a story, or recount an experience with appropriate facts and relevant, descriptive details, speaking clearly at an understandable pace.	Report on a topic or text, tell a story, or recount an experience in an organized manner, using appropriate facts and relevant, descriptive details to support main ideas or themes; speak clearly at an understandable pace.	Report on a topic or text or present an opinion, sequencing ideas logically and using appropriate facts and relevant, descriptive details to support main ideas or themes; speak clearly at an understandable pace.
5	Add drawings or other visual displays to descriptions as desired to provide additional detail.	Add drawings or other visual displays to descriptions when appropriate to clarify ideas, thoughts, and feelings.	Create audio recordings of stories or poems; add drawings or other visual displays to stories or recounts of experiences when appropriate to clarify ideas, thoughts, and feelings.	Create engaging audio recordings of stories or poems that demonstrate fluid reading at an understandable pace; add visual displays when appropriate to emphasize or enhance certain facts or details.	Add audio recordings and visual displays to presentations when appropriate to enhance the development of main ideas or themes.	Include multimedia components (e.g., graphics, sound) and visual displays in presentations when appropriate to enhance the development of main ideas or themes.
6	Speak audibly and express thoughts, feelings, and ideas clearly.	Produce complete sentences when appropriate to task and situation.	Produce complete sentences when appropriate to task and situation in order to provide requested detail or clarification.	Speak in complete sentences when appropriate to task and situation in order to provide requested detail or clarification.	Differentiate between contexts that call for formal English (e.g., presenting ideas) and situations where informal discourse is appropriate (e.g., small-group discussion); use formal English when appropriate to task and situation.	Adapt speech to a variety of contexts and tasks, using formal English when appropriate to task and situation.

These text types should not be confused with different forms of texts, which include essays, science journal entries, reports, and letters. While students in the early grades write mostly within a single text type (narrative, informational, or persuasive), in the hands of older writers, some of these products may call for two or three of the text types. For example, a report may include an opening scenario (narrative text type) followed by factual information (explanatory/informational text type) and concluding with a persuasive section on the next steps a reader can take (argumentation text type). The use of these text types varies according to the form, but all three require the use of a strong organizational structure so that ideas, concepts, events, and reasons flow in a way that other readers can understand them.

Paralleling the research standards in the reading domain, **standards 7, 8, and 9** concern themselves with children's ability to participate in teacher-directed and shared investigative projects. The research sources should include those that represent a breadth and depth of print, digital, and multimedia texts and that rely on evidence from those sources to support ideas presented in their writing. A table detailing the writing standards is located in Figure 5.4.

Figure 5.4 ELA Writing Standards That Focus on *What the Text Inspires You to Do*

	Kindergarten	Grade 1	Grade 2	Grade 3	Grade 4	Grade 5
1	Use a combination of drawing, dictating, and writing to compose opinion pieces in which they tell a reader the topic or the name of the book they are writing about and state an opinion or preference about the book.	Write opinion pieces in which they introduce the topic or name the book they are writing about, state an opinion, supply a reason for the opinion, and provide some sense of closure.	Write opinion pieces in which they introduce the topic or book they are writing about, state an opinion, supply reasons that support the opinion, use linking words (e.g., *because, and, also*) to connect opinion and reasons, and provide a concluding statement or section.	Write opinion pieces on topics or texts, supporting a point of view with reasons. a. Introduce the topic or text they are writing about, state an opinion, and create an organizational structure that lists reasons. b. Provide reasons that support the opinion. c. Use linking words and phrases (e.g., *because, therefore, since, for example*) to connect opinion and reasons. d. Provide a concluding statement or section.	Write opinion pieces on topics or texts, supporting a point of view with reasons and information. a. Introduce a topic or text clearly, state an opinion, and create an organizational structure in which related ideas are grouped to support the writer's purpose. b. Provide reasons that are supported by facts and details. c. Link opinion and reasons using words and phrases (e.g., for instance, in order to, in addition). d. Provide a concluding statement or section related to the opinion presented.	Write opinion pieces on topics or texts, supporting a point of view with reasons and information. a. Introduce a topic or text clearly, state an opinion, and create an organizational structure in which ideas are logically grouped to support the writer's purpose. b. Provide logically ordered reasons that are supported by facts and details. c. Link opinion and reasons using words, phrases, and clauses (e.g., consequently, specifically). d. Provide a concluding statement or section related to the opinion presented.

	Kindergarten	Grade 1	Grade 2	Grade 3	Grade 4	Grade 5
2	Use a combination of drawing, dictating, and writing to compose informative/explanatory texts in which they name what they are writing about and supply some information about the topic.	Write informative/explanatory texts in which they name a topic, supply some facts about the topic, and provide some sense of closure.	Write informative/explanatory texts in which they introduce a topic, use facts and definitions to develop points, and provide a concluding statement or section.	Write informative/explanatory texts to examine a topic and convey ideas and information clearly. a. Introduce a topic and group related information together; include illustrations when useful to aiding comprehension. b. Develop the topic with facts, definitions, and details. c. Use linking words and phrases (e.g., *also, another, and, more, but*) to connect ideas within categories of information. d. Provide a concluding statement or section.	Write informative/explanatory texts to examine a topic and convey ideas and information clearly. a. Introduce a topic clearly and group related information in paragraphs and sections; include formatting (e.g., headings), illustrations, and multimedia when useful to aiding comprehension. b. Develop the topic with facts, definitions, concrete details, quotations, or other information and examples related to the topic. c. Link ideas within categories of information using words and phrases (e.g., *another, for example, also, because*).	Write informative/explanatory texts to examine a topic and convey ideas and information clearly. a. Introduce a topic clearly, provide a general observation and focus, and group related information logically; include formatting (e.g., headings), illustrations, and multimedia when useful to aiding comprehension. b. Develop the topic with facts, definitions, concrete details, quotations, or other information and examples related to the topic. c. Link ideas within and across categories of information using words, phrases, and clauses (e.g., *in contrast, especially*).

(Continued)

Figure 5.4 (Continued)

	Kindergarten	Grade 1	Grade 2	Grade 3	Grade 4	Grade 5
					d. Use precise language and domain-specific vocabulary to inform about or explain the topic. e. Provide a concluding statement or section related to the information or explanation presented.	d. Use precise language and domain-specific vocabulary to inform about or explain the topic. e. Provide a concluding statement or section related to the information or explanation presented.
3	Use a combination of drawing, dictating, and writing to narrate a single event or several loosely linked events, tell about the events in the order in which they occurred, and provide a reaction to what happened.	Write narratives in which they recount two or more appropriately sequenced events, include some details regarding what happened, use temporal words to signal event order, and provide some sense of closure.	Write narratives in which they recount a well-elaborated event or short sequence of events, include details to describe actions, thoughts, and feelings, use temporal words to signal event order, and provide a sense of closure.	Write narratives to develop real or imagined experiences or events using effective technique, descriptive details, and clear event sequences. a. Establish a situation and introduce a narrator and/or characters; organize an event sequence that unfolds naturally.	Write narratives to develop real or imagined experiences or events using effective technique, descriptive details, and clear event sequences. a. Orient the reader by establishing a situation and introducing a narrator and/or characters; organize an event sequence that unfolds naturally.	Write narratives to develop real or imagined experiences or events using effective technique, descriptive details, and clear event sequences. a. Orient the reader by establishing a situation and introducing a narrator and/or characters; organize an event sequence that unfolds naturally.

Kindergarten	Grade 1	Grade 2	Grade 3	Grade 4	Grade 5
			b. Use dialogue and descriptions of actions, thoughts, and feelings to develop experiences and events or show the response of characters to situations. c. Use temporal words and phrases to signal event order. d. Provide a sense of closure.	b. Use dialogue and description to develop experiences and events or show the responses of characters to situations. c. Use a variety of transitional words and phrases to manage the sequence of events. d. Use concrete words and phrases and sensory details to convey experiences and events precisely. e. Provide a conclusion that follows from the narrated experiences or events.	b. Use narrative techniques, such as dialogue, description, and pacing, to develop experiences and events or show the responses of characters to situations. c. Use a variety of transitional words, phrases, and clauses to manage the sequence of events. d. Use concrete words and phrases and sensory details to convey experiences and events precisely. e. Provide a conclusion that follows from the narrated experiences or events.

(Continued)

Figure 5.4 (Continued)

	Kindergarten	Grade 1	Grade 2	Grade 3	Grade 4	Grade 5
7	Participate in shared research and writing projects (e.g., explore a number of books by a favorite author and express opinions about them).	Participate in shared research and writing projects (e.g., explore a number of "how-to" books on a given topic and use them to write a sequence of instructions).	Participate in shared research and writing projects (e.g., read a number of books on a single topic to produce a report; record science observations).	Conduct short research projects that build knowledge about a topic.	Conduct short research projects that build knowledge through investigation of different aspects of a topic.	Conduct short research projects that use several sources to build knowledge through investigation of different aspects of a topic.
8	With guidance and support from adults, recall information from experiences or gather information from provided sources to answer a question.	With guidance and support from adults, recall information from experiences or gather information from provided sources to answer a question.	Recall information from experiences or gather information from provided sources to answer a question.	Recall information from experiences or gather information from print and digital sources; take brief notes on sources and sort evidence into provided categories.	Recall relevant information from experiences or gather relevant information from print and digital sources; take notes and categorize information, and provide a list of sources.	Recall relevant information from experiences or gather relevant information from print and digital sources; summarize or paraphrase information in notes and finished work, and provide a list of sources.
9	(Begins in grade 4)	(Begins in grade 4)	(Begins in grade 4)	(Begins in grade 4)	Draw evidence from literary or informational texts to support analysis, reflection, and research. a. Apply grade 4 Reading standards to literature (e.g., "Describe in depth a character, setting, or event in a story or drama,	Draw evidence from literary or informational texts to support analysis, reflection, and research. a. Apply grade 5 Reading standards to literature (e.g., "Compare and contrast two or more characters, settings, or events in a story

Kindergarten	Grade 1	Grade 2	Grade 3	Grade 4	Grade 5
				drawing on specific details in the text [e.g., a character's thoughts, words, or actions]."). b. Apply grade 4 Reading standards to informational texts (e.g., "Explain how an author uses reasons and evidence to support particular points in a text").	or a drama, drawing on specific details in the text [e.g., how characters interact]"). b. Apply grade 5 Reading standards to informational texts (e.g., "Explain how an author uses reasons and evidence to support particular points in a text, identifying which reasons and evidence support which point[s]").

Using Text-Dependent Tasks About
What the Text Inspires You to Do

There are a number of different tasks that teachers can use to check for understanding. These tasks provide students an opportunity to demonstrate their thinking about the text under investigation. Importantly, these tasks often allow students to understand the text, and the ideas surrounding the text, in a much more comprehensive way. But even more importantly, these tasks all demand that students cite textual evidence in their products. In other words, students have to understand *what the text says*, *how the text works*, and *what the text means*, if they are going to be successful with these tasks.

As the adage notes, you don't always know what you think until you write it down. The same can be said for the development of a presentation; the preparation for a test, seminar, or debate; or the investigation of a claim or topic. In essence, these tasks show students that the close reading they have done is worthy of their time. Students use their annotations, ideas, and collaborative conversations in service of the task that allows them to make the text their own.

> These tasks show students that the close reading they have done is worthy of their time. Students use their annotations, ideas, and collaborative conversations in service of the task that allows them to make the text their own.

Presentations

Say the word *presentation,* and most people think immediately of a set of slides and a clicker. But presentations are first and foremost about being able to explain a set of ideas to an audience of listeners. As noted in speaking and listening **standard 5**, students are expected to develop and hone their presentation skills, especially in terms of being able to relay information about an event or topic. In the primary grades, children are offering such accounts and supporting their presentations with visuals, often drawings or illustrations. By second grade, the range of support features expands to the creation of audio recordings. Students in grades 3–5 should have the opportunity to develop short, organized presentations that also expand their public speaking skills. The presentations they develop should be factually accurate and can include a variety of multimedia components (e.g., graphics, images, music, sound) and visual displays. Of course, we know that speaking before a group remains the number one fear for the majority of people (Wallechinsky, Wallace, & Wallace, 1977). Hopefully, if students have a lot of practice with presentations while they are younger, we can overcome this social phobia.

Effective presentations are those that have good content and are delivered well. This requires that students engage in shared research to locate information, which in and of itself is challenging. Haeffner (2006) developed a project entitled "Wouldn't It Be Cool?" (for example, "wouldn't it be cool to sing like an opera star?") for classroom teachers and library media specialists to use jointly to assist second and third grade students to develop speeches. Children identified a topic and conducted their research using how-to informational books. They used the following outline to develop their speech (p. 23):

I.   Your topic:

II.   Why would it be fun and exciting to be a _____?

III.   What are the skills needed?

IV.   How do you learn the skills needed?

V.   What does it take to do it well?

VI.   Wouldn't it be cool to be a _____?

Many of the skills associated with speaking in public have to do with outward behaviors, such as maintaining a sufficient volume so that listeners can hear, using eye contact to connect with the audience, and using gestures that enhance rather than distract from the message. Figure 5.5 is an oral presentation rubric for grades 3–12 that outlines expectations for both the delivery and content of a speech or presentation. Of course, these should be taught and practiced in advance.

It is important that listeners also actively participate in speeches and presentations. We're leery, however, of peer feedback that focuses exclusively on the delivery, with little attention given to the content of the message. As listeners, children need experience with extracting information from a presentation as well as posing questions. We like to structure peer feedback of student presentations so that they identify strengths, ask a question, and make a suggestion.

For example, the students in Greta Wilkie's fourth grade class listened to presentations their classmates had developed and delivered concerning the history of Native American tribes in their state. Students

Figure 5.5 Speech and Presentation Rubric

	4—Excellent	3—Good	2—Fair	1—Needs Improvement	
Delivery	• Holds attention of entire audience with the use of direct eye contact, seldom looking at notes • Speaks with fluctuation in volume and inflection to maintain audience interest and emphasize key points	• Consistent use of direct eye contact with audience, but still returns to notes • Speaks with satisfactory variation of volume and inflection	• Displays minimal eye contact with audience, while reading mostly from the notes • Speaks in uneven volume with little or no inflection	• Holds no eye contact with audience, as entire report is read from notes • Speaks in low volume and/or monotonous tone, which causes audience to disengage	
Content and Organization	• Demonstrates full knowledge by answering all class questions with explanations and elaboration • Provides clear purpose and subject; pertinent examples, facts, and/or statistics; supports conclusions/ideas with evidence	• Is at ease with expected answers to all questions, without elaboration • Has somewhat clear purpose and subject; some examples, facts, and/or statistics that support the subject; includes some data or evidence that supports conclusions	• Is uncomfortable with information and is able to answer only rudimentary questions • Attempts to define purpose and subject; provides weak examples, facts, and/or statistics, which do not adequately support the subject; includes very thin data or evidence	• Does not have grasp of information and cannot answer questions about subject • Does not clearly define subject and purpose; provides weak or no support of subject; gives insufficient support for ideas or conclusions	
Enthusiasm and Audience Awareness	• Demonstrates strong enthusiasm about topic during entire presentation • Significantly increases audience understanding and knowledge of topic; convinces an audience to recognize the validity and importance of the subject	• Shows some enthusiastic feelings about topic • Raises audience understanding and awareness of most points	• Shows little or mixed feelings about the topic being presented • Raises audience understanding and knowledge of some points	• Shows no interest in topic presented • Fails to increase audience understanding of knowledge of topic	
Comments					

Source: www.readwritethink.org/classroom-resources/printouts/oral-presentation-rubric-30700.html investigated one of nine different tribes and then made short presentations to the class. In turn, each student listener was tasked with providing feedback to fellow presenters. Each day, five students presented and then met with a small group of peers to debrief the presentation. Listeners used a simple form developed by the teacher (see Figure 5.6) to frame the discussion.

"Each presenter meets with five listeners who come to the table prepared for the discussion," said Ms. Wilkie. "They're accountable to each other and to the material. I think the most valuable part for the presenters and the listeners is the discussion about the questions. When they know they need to come up with a thought-provoking question, it really puts them on their toes," she said.

Writing From Sources

All writing should have purpose, and these purposes fall into three categories: (1) to convey an experience, real or imagined; (2) to inform or explain an event, process, or phenomenon; and (3) to persuade. These purposes correlate to the three major text types: narrative, informational/explanatory, and opinion with evidence.

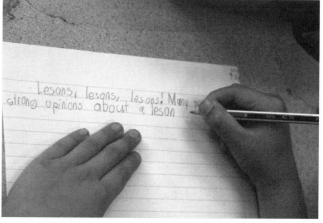

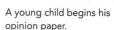
A young child begins his opinion paper.

The challenge is that too often young writers are invited by us to turn their attention away from the text we as teachers have worked so hard to help them understand deeply. Instead, we ask them to "write about a time when someone challenged you to participate in a fight" rather than turn them back to the speech delivered by Patrick Henry. To be clear, it is not as though their personal experiences are without value to us. In fact, their ability to convey such an experience and ground it in the context of one or more readings makes the writing more powerful. But we need to be mindful of how our writing prompts can lead them away from texts, thereby robbing them of the opportunity to engage in the kind of critical thinking that moves them from text interpretation (*what the text means*) to action (*what the text inspires you to do*).

Figure 5.6   Peer Feedback and Discussion Form

Your Name: _____   Name of Speaker: _____

Title of Presentation: _____

A STRENGTH: My favorite part of your presentation was

It was my favorite part because

A THOUGHT-PROVOKING QUESTION: A question I have about the information you presented is

The answer to my question is

AN IDEA: One suggestion I have for your next presentation is

We have found the task templates developed by the Literacy Design Collaborative (LDC) (www.literacydesigncollaborative.org) to be immensely helpful for crafting writing prompts such that readers reference the text and cite evidence to support their points. The LDC task templates work for teachers in much the same way that sentence frames work for students, because they provide an academic language frame for original ideas. For instance, task template 6 from the grades 4–5 collection reads:

> [Insert optional question.] After reading [literary or informational text/s] write a/an [product] in which you describe [content]. Give [an, several, or #] example/s from [text/s] to support your discussion.

Xavier Mendoza used the above task template from LDC to design a writing prompt for his third grade students:

> How do characters meet the challenge of being in an unfamiliar place? After reading "Marven of the Great North Woods," write an essay in which you describe Marven's challenges and how he reacted to them. Give three examples from the text to support your discussion.

"This book [Lasky, 1997] is all about the resilience of this young boy from Minnesota whose family has been struck down by the flu epidemic of 1918," the teacher explained. "The boy, Marven, strikes out for a logging camp and goes to work there. Against all the odds, and with the support of one of the lumberjacks, Marven succeeds. I want to make sure they get the chance to really admire what this kid accomplished in the face of great odds," said Mr. Mendoza. "This is based on a true story, and we'll be using this as a foundation for examining the resiliency of characters throughout the year."

Socratic Seminars

One specific type of discussion and analysis of a text is called a Socratic seminar, which is defined as a "collaborative, intellectual dialogue facilitated with open-ended questions about the text" (Roberts & Billings, 2012, p. 22). Students read and annotate the text in advance of the Socratic seminar, either in class or outside of class. In addition to reading the text, students write a short, reflective piece in advance of the Socratic seminar, addressing a question posed by the teacher or their peers. Typically, the question focuses on general understandings and key details (*what the text says*). Deeper understandings of the text emerge during the seminar as students use their knowledge about *how the text works* and *what it means* as they interact with others.

There are four components of a Socratic seminar:

1. *The text,* which should be selected because it is worthy of investigation and discussion.

2. *The questions,* which should lead participants back to the text as they speculate, evaluate, define, and clarify the issues involved.

3. *The leader,* who is both guide and participant. The leader, who can be a student or the teacher, helps participants clarify their positions, involves reluctant participants, and restrains overactive members of the group.

4. *The participants,* who come to the discussion having read the text, ready to share their ideas and perspectives with others.

Some of the questions that students might struggle with during a Socratic seminar include these:

- Could you give me an example or a metaphor to explain that?

- Can you find that in the text?

- Where does the reading support you?

- What are you assuming in that argument?

- What is the author's perspective, and how does this inform the message?

- Why is [word or phrase] pivotal to understanding this text?

- Is [concept] a good thing or a bad thing?

- What evidence in the text helps us understand whether the writer would agree or disagree with [concept]?

- What does [phrase or sentence] mean in the context of this reading?

- Where does the turning point in this piece occur, and why is it important?

- In what ways does our understanding of [character] depend on the [thoughts/actions/dialogue] of others?

- What is the theme of this text? What is your evidence?

- How does this text align or contrast with [previously read text]? (adapted from Fisher & Frey, 2014b)

In each case, the text is important, and students learn that they need to have read and understood the text to participate.

First grade teacher Taylor Kittridge uses a form of Socratic seminar to build the habit of extended discussion with her young students. "I want them to get accustomed to the idea that from time to time we'll all come together to talk about something, and that I'm not going to be the traffic cop," Ms. Kittridge said. "By first grade they're already used to talking to the teacher, but not each other. This helps me to reinforce how groups engage in discussion." The class had read and discussed the picture book *Encounter* (Yolen, 1992) and had written and illustrated a short piece about the young Taino Indian's attempts to warn his elders about the dangers of welcoming the explorers into their midst. This set the stage for their discussion about alternative perspectives on the familiar story of Columbus's discovery of the New World. Students and their teacher sat in a circle, and Ms. Kittridge posed a series of questions asking them to compare and contrast the differences between the two accounts.

"I keep it pretty simple for them at this age," she explained later. "We do this as a 15-minute discussion, and my role is mostly to remind them to use their writing and the texts in their discussion. They've got the materials in front of them, so everyone can find them," she said. "I think what's most important at this age is how I stage the classroom. Because I am sitting in the circle with them, they are learning to talk to each other, not just to me. Since it's the second half of the year, I am now assigning the role of the leader to a child, who asks the questions of the group."

Debates

Similar to a Socratic seminar, debates require that students carefully analyze texts such that they can use evidence from the texts to make a case effectively. In a debate, students need to carefully examine an issue, research both sides of the issue, and be prepared to defend a position. Importantly, learning the skills of debate can improve student achievement and engagement in school (Mezuk, Bondarenko, Smith, & Tucker, 2011). In part, this is because students must read more widely than the assigned texts in order to be successful. To effectively debate, students must understand a wide range of texts and be able to use those texts strategically. In addition, these achievement gains can be partially attributed to the development of oral language skills that takes place as students learn to engage in interactions with one another. And finally, these strides in achievement can be partially attributed to the depth of understanding required of students to engage in the debate itself. As Mezuk, Bondarenko, Smith, and Tucker (2011) noted, this is "particularly relevant in light of the new Common Core State Standards . . . [which] focus on evidence-based argument and informational text mastery as critical language arts skills" (p. 630).

As part of the debate process, students rely on texts for evidence. In preparing for debates, students read and reread several texts, taking notes that they can use later. During the debate, students use their resources to argue in a structured way. Of course, students have to understand the rules of a debate. Typically, a team debate has different phases, such as the following:

- Pro—Someone presents the "for" position.

- Con—Someone presents the "against" position.

- Pro—Someone presents evidence related to the "for" position.

- Con—Someone presents evidence related to the "against" position.

- Pro—Someone refutes the evidence from the "against" position.

- Con—Someone refutes the evidence from the "for" position.

- Pro—Someone salvages the most persuasive arguments left and makes a concluding statement.

- Con—Someone salvages the most persuasive arguments left and makes a concluding statement.

> Learning the skills of debate can improve student achievement and engagement in school.

Typically, the judge reviews the proceedings and declares a debate winner. Figure 5.7 contains debate guidelines developed by Heather Anderson. As with other tasks that students must be taught, the rules of debate and the ways in which debates are conducted are important considerations for teachers. There are a number of resources about effective debate skills (e.g., Edwards, 2008; Marzano, Pickering, & Heflebower, 2011).

At the elementary level, students have to learn that a debate does not mean a fight or argument. Often, teachers provide some general rules for the debate. For example, a teacher might list some Debate Do's and Don'ts on chart paper in the room as students learn to engage their peers in this way, such as the following:

- Stay calm and focused. Don't yell or lose your temper!

- Use evidence from texts. Don't use personal stories as examples for your arguments.

- Pay attention to the details from the other group. Don't ignore the arguments from the other team.

- Follow the format of the debate carefully. Don't veer from the structure of the debate and argue randomly.

- Make it fun. Don't make it personal or take it personally.

"We sure have had lots of fun with this!" laughed fifth grade teacher Jerry Yee. "Our first debate of the year was really just kind of light, so they'd get used to the format. We debated the relative merits of homework. You can guess how that one went!"

Since Mr. Yee introduced the debate format to students, the topics have gotten more serious. "We had a great one on whether limiting screen time was a good idea or not, and another where they debated some pending state legislation to remove unhealthy snacks from school vending machines," he said. "In each case, it was the research they had to do that made it really valuable."

Mr. Yee's fifth grade social studies curriculum is about American history to 1850, so the last debate of the year is the most formal one yet. "I'm using the topic developed by the Atlanta Urban Debate Society for its elementary competition: 'Resolved: Conflict is

Figure 5.7   Debate Guidelines

Each team of four will have two people on the affirmative (for) side and two people on the negative (against) side.

Debate Format

1. Affirmative (for) presents case: three minutes max

2. Negative (against) presents case: three minutes max

3. Affirmative (for) and negative (against) respond to one another: four minutes max each

4. Affirmative (for) summarizes and concludes: one minute max

5. Negative (against) summarizes and concludes: one minute max

After the debate, the class will vote to see which side won. This vote will not influence your final grade.

Tips

1. **You are always right.** No matter what you really believe, if you want to win, then you have to believe that whatever you say is correct, and your opposition is always wrong.

2. **Strong central argument.** Every point you make should be linked back to this central argument.

3. **Rebut.** If the other side states an incorrect fact, rebut it. If they do not link back to their team's case, rebut it. If they give an example that has no relevance, rebut it. Remember, the opposition is always wrong.

4. **Never insult the opposition.** No matter how much you want to, don't! If you want to insult something, do it to their argument. Don't use personal attacks if you want to win.

5. **Have passion.** Believe in what you are saying, and you probably will win. Speak from the heart, but also use logic and research.

Debate Sentence Frames

I will argue that. . . .	I will show that. . . .	You can see that. . . .
The evidence shows that. . . .	My opponent believes. . . .	All the evidence points toward. . . .
That is simply not true. . . .	It is clear that. . . .	My opponent is wrong because. . . .

Available for download from **www.corwin.com/textdependentquestions**

necessary for the betterment of U.S. society.'" (Find out more about this tournament at http://atlantadebate.org/elementary-school-debate.) Mr. Yee intends for his students to use the lens of conflict in US history to examine the pros and cons of this statement. "This isn't an easy question for them to tackle, and I'm looking forward to seeing how they will use what they've learned this year to support their claims," he said.

Investigations

Sometimes the texts that are used for close reading generate a lot of additional questions for students. In essence, these texts inspire students to find things out. In these cases, an appropriate task is an investigation. As we have noted before, investigations can be short or long. Students are expected to "conduct short as well as more sustained research projects based on focused questions, demonstrating understanding of the subject under investigation" (CCSSI, 2010a, p. 41). In addition, students are asked to integrate information from a range of diverse sources. This requires that they find additional resources, print or digital, that they can use to inform their research or explain the topic under investigation.

Like students over 100 years ago, our students today must identify sources, take notes, and synthesize information (Pfaffinger, 2006). The expectations of an information report haven't changed, but the way students go about completing the task has. Students can now use technology to complete their papers. They can Google, e-mail, highlight, cut and paste, and use all kinds of tools that make the work of writing their report easier and faster. We have organized these new strategies into four distinct categories that can be taught (Frey, Fisher, & Gonzalez, 2010):

- **Finding Information.** To effectively transform knowledge to understanding, students need varied approaches, tools, and vocabulary for finding information. They need to be taught how to search for information as well as how to evaluate the credibility of the information that they find.

- **Using Information.** Once students have collected information, they need accessible ways to keep it organized. From note cards to class notes, common tools have developed into

> The expectations of an information report haven't changed, but the way students go about completing the task has.

digital versions that can save time and improve the organizational quality. In addition, students need to be taught how to cite the sources they use and not plagiarize information.

- **Producing Information.** As part of the investigation process, students must synthesize the information they find and present that information in their own words with their own organizational system. This requires a great deal of practice and students deserve feedback from their peers and teachers as they approximate success with this.

- **Sharing Information.** Producing an essay has been the end point for many students. When students submit their paper, having found and used good information, it's fairly anticlimatic. They have worked so hard and learned so much, and there their newfound knowledge sits, in a paper in the teacher's backpack. Today's students want more. Producing is not enough for students in the 21st century. They want to share their information. This need to share may be the result of students' exposure to countless YouTube videos, blog postings, tweets, Facebook status updates, or something else, but the fact remains that our students want to share.

The kindergarten students in Keisha Short's class participated in a shared investigation on weather. They read and discussed a number of texts, including selected passages from *Weather* (Simon, 1993). As part of their investigation, they monitored and reported on the local conditions each day. "I didn't want them gathering data just by opening the classroom door and saying, 'It's sunny' or whatever," said Ms. Short. Instead, they watched the local weather forecast on the Internet each morning and recorded the high and low temperatures and precipitation from the previous day. Because it was tornado season at the time, they consulted books and online resources about tornados and how to protect themselves in case of emergency. "We did this for a month," said Ms. Short, "so we really had some nice data. Together we composed a class book about our local weather, including the monthly rainfall, range of temperatures, and numbers of sunny and cloudy days," she said. "We also wrote about what we had learned about tornadoes and safety measures."

But Ms. Short had more to offer about this. "I've done this weather project for several years, but I was always the one who decided what resources we should use," she said. "This year I made sure to take the time to capture their questions about weather, which shaped the direction of the investigation. We did a lot more with tornadoes this year, because that's what they wanted to learn about." She also linked this to conducting searches on the Internet. "This has been a great way to have conversations about keywords in searches, like what terms we should be looking for," the kindergarten teacher said. "I'm doing the typing, but I'm projecting my screen, so they can see what I'm doing. For our next investigation, which will involve engineering and building little vehicles that move under wind power, we'll put our results on our classroom wiki."

Tests

Summative assessments of students' understanding are another task that can be used to determine whether or not students understand a text. Although there are a number of formats for test questions, the ones that interest us for the purpose of close reading are those that involve the use of evidence from the text in order to determine the answer. In other words, we are less interested in recall-of-information questions when we are using tests as a task related to close reading. We are interested in questions that encourage the reader to return to the text to determine whether the evidence supports the answer. We are also interested in questions that require students to provide evidence from the text itself.

We are less interested in recall-of-information questions when we are using tests as a task related to close reading. We are interested in questions that encourage the reader to return to the text to determine whether the evidence supports the answer.

Good tests allow teachers to understand students' thinking. Incorrect responses are not just random collections of answers but rather inform the teacher about students' misunderstanding. These diagnostic distractors, even on a summative assessment, can be used to guide the instruction teachers provide later in the year.

For example, the second grade students in Hector Moreno's class took short online comprehension quizzes that came with his reading program. "Honestly, I didn't always do these, because I thought it was something I didn't have time for," he said. "But with the growth of online testing beginning in third grade, I realized that I needed to build some skills among my students to test in this environment."

The publisher's quizzes were mostly questions that were focused on literal-level meaning (in other words, what the text says), but Mr. Moreno was able to customize the tests to include higher-level questions. "It's giving them lots of practice in seeing how those kinds of questions show up in lots of different places," he said. "It also gives me a chance to see what they know when the task is different. I'm not grading them, but I am looking at the results, so I can see how well they are able to answer when the task is an independent one."

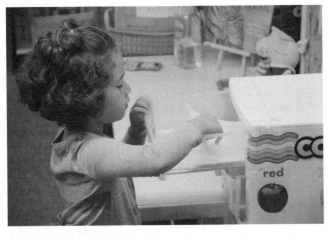

A kindergartener prepares to write.

Examples of What the Text Inspired

What the Text Inspired in Kindergarten and First Grade

The students in Steve Bradley's kindergarten classroom had come to the end of their discussion about Chapter 2 of *Winnie-the-Pooh* (Milne, 1926). Mr. Bradley invited his students to write about their understanding of the text. He had developed a prompt that accommodated the wide range of writing skills in his classroom. He read the prompt aloud from the document camera:

What do friends do? After listening to, and discussing, the chapter from *Winnie-the-Pooh*, write and draw an example that explains how one friend helped or didn't help Pooh.

Returning to their desks, the students took out their writing journals and opened to a new page. They knew that they were allowed to check their responses with peers and that they were expected to produce text.

Hunter, turning to Kiara, said, "I wanna write about Rabbit. He tried to help but it didn't work. He said Winnie-the-Pooh ate too much and that's not nice."

"I'm gonna draw Christopher Robin reading a book," Kiara responded. "He helped because Winnie-the-Pooh was stuck."

Mr. Bradley moved from table to table, checking his students' work. He noted that Chase was drawing a group of people on playground equipment. Mr. Bradley asked Chase about his work, saying, *"You have a lot of details in your work. Can you tell me about it?"*

Chase responded, "It's friends at recess. They're sharing the ball and swings."

"I see that. That's a great thing for friends to do. I wonder if Pooh's friends did that. I don't remember that from the book, do you?"

"No; it's my friends," Chase responded.

"Oh, I see. Would it be possible for you to work on a new paper for our writing prompt about Winnie-the-Pooh and what his friends did or did not do and then come back to finish this one? We could even compare the actions of Winnie-the-Pooh's friends and your friends in our circle after this, if you want."

Chase, looking up at his teacher, said, "Okay. Sounds good." And just that quickly, he grabbed a new piece of paper and starting drawing small circles in a row.

Mr. Bradley, wanting to check that this was more connected with the prompt, said, *"That's interesting. What's that?"* To which Chase responded, "It's gonna be all of Rabbit's friends who came to help pull."

What the Text Inspired in Second and Third Grades

Following their investigation of peer pressure, including a website review and the reading of two books, the students in Sonia Perez's second and third grade combination class were asked to respond to a writing prompt based on the task templates introduced by the Literacy Design Collaborative (www.literacydesigncollaborative .com):

> After reading the informational website, *Hey, Little Ant,* and *A Bad Case of the Stripes,* write a short essay in which you explain the causes and the effects of peer pressure and/or bullying. Give several examples from the texts to support your discussion.

The students started working on this task as Ms. Perez met with a small group of students who had experienced difficulty during the last writing task. She began the conversation asking each of them how they planned to start.

Marco was first to respond, saying, "I'm gonna say what it is first 'cuz last time that's what you said, that I didn't tell what I was writing about first."

"Do you mean that you're going to explain peer pressure or bullying first?" Ms. Perez asked.

"Yes," Marco responded.

"Nice. That's one of the things that we noticed about writers that we like to read, remember? They give us some information about the topic to start. I think your readers will really appreciate this," Ms. Perez said.

After the other students then shared their ideas, Ms. Perez turned their attention back to the use of evidence. *"I want us to remember that evidence from the text helps writers make their claims more believable. We've talked about this before, as a whole class, so I'm just reminding you now. You might want to think about the evidence that you'll use. Maybe you even want to write down the evidence you'll use. That could help you with the flow and organization of your papers. It seems that you're all ready to write. Is that true?* [the students nod affirmatively] *I look forward to seeing your drafts. I'll meet with you all in about 15 or 20 minutes to see where you are."*

Ms. Perez then called another group of students over to her table. This time, she met with the strongest writers in the class and engaged them in a conversation about their use of linking words to alert the reader to shifts and upcoming information. As she said, *"I wanted to remind you of the analysis we did last time we met. Remember when we looked at several pieces of text and highlighted the signal words? Well, I made a list of the words you all found. You can glue this into your writer's notebook. And look at the amount of space that I left so that you could add new signal words as you learn them or as you find them in the things you read."* The students spent a few minutes talking about the signal words, and then they traded drafts and made recommendations about places their peers could provide some advanced organization for the readers.

Ms. Perez continued to meet with students, individually and in small groups, as they drafted their responses to the prompt. When the time came for the lesson to end, Ms. Perez said to the class, *"I think that many of you are nearly done with your drafts. You can work on this some more later today when you have finished your other 'must do' tasks. Or you can work on it in the after-school program or at home. Remember, we're going to have a longer conversation about recommendations for the charac-*

A teacher confers with a group of students about their writing.

ters in two days, so I'd like us to be clear about the causes and effects of peer pressure and bullying before we do so."

Two days later, when the time came for their Socratic seminar, the students in Ms. Perez's class had all completed at least a draft and one revision of their papers. They had engaged in peer feedback and had received comments from their teacher. In other words, they were prepared for a longer conversation about the topics of bullying and peer pressure.

The students were seated in a large circle, and Ms. Perez began the whole class discussion, saying, *"Welcome to our Socratic seminar. We all know the rules for this conversation, and I have them posted on the wall behind Joseph. For our opening question, I'd like us to talk about recommendations for the boy in* Hey, Little Ant *and the girl in* A Bad Case of Stripes. *As part of the conversation, I hope we talk about the causes of their respective situations and what the effects were and could be."*

The students engaged in a 35-minute discussion in which they analyzed the role of peers in both characters' lives. They also noted that bullying involved bystanders, and both of the books included that aspect. Their conversation remained focused on the books, with evidence being drawn from the illustrations and words. Their conversation ended with a class pact—an agreement that they would try their best not to bully others and to recognize it when it was happening and then ask for help. Ms. Perez was pleased with her students' level of understanding and the products they created that allowed her to assess both their literacy development and their social skills.

What the Text Inspired in Fourth and Fifth Grades

The students in Ms. Washington's fifth grade class had been working in groups for several weeks when they read the speech delivered by Patrick Henry. Following their close reading of the text, Ms. Washington asked her students to return to their groups and to discuss their assigned colony's response to the speech.

"You probably can't just Google this," she said. *"You have to really think about what you know about your colony. Who lives there? What did they generally believe? Would they have supported the fight with England, or did they have too much to lose? What you can do is use your research to discuss this and look for more evidence to hypothesize the level of support in the given colony."*

The students opened their iPads and laptops while they talked about their understanding of their colony. The group assigned to Massachusetts started talking about the support for the Revolutionary War. As Noah said, "Our colony was all about going to war. It says right here that in February 1775, Massachusetts was in rebellion. Even before the speech, they were already starting to fight with the British."

"What I found was that in April, the British commander was told to disarm the rebels and arrest their leaders," Zoe added. "So, I agree with Noah that our colony was totally about independence and was going to join the fight against British rule."

Ms. Washington provided her students with about 15 minutes to conduct their research before interrupting them. *"We're going to do another Pecha Kucha (www.pechakucha.org) style presentation. Each group gets 20 slides, and each slide will auto-advance in 20 seconds. That means you only get a total of just over six minutes to make your case. Your presentation should include information about your colony, including its location, as well as the general political climate at the time, March 1775. You should clearly indicate whether or not your group believes that the colonists would support Patrick Henry and his call for war with England.*

Also, remember to include your sources in the speakers' notes so that I can check your evidence."

The students had created these presentations in the past, and they knew that they needed powerful images to make their points. They also knew that they needed to be very clear on the content for each slide, because the slides would move quickly; 20 seconds is not a lot of time to talk. As Tamara reminded her group, "Remember that we can put the same image in twice, if we need more time on some information."

"Oh yeah, good point," Marcus responded. "Who wants to do which parts? I'd like to do the location and description of the people, if that's okay. But we gotta get this done so that we can practice and make changes once we all see it."

QUESTION YOURSELF

This chapter has focused on tasks that require students to use the texts they have read to demonstrate their understanding. More specifically, these tasks allow students to respond to the question, "What does the text mean to me, and what does it inspire me to do?" The level of thinking required in these tasks assumes students know *what the text says, how the text works,* and *what the text means.* The range of tasks includes presentations, writing from sources, Socratic seminars, debates, research and investigation, and tests.

Now we invite you to test yourself. We have included a summary of the Bill of Rights (Figure 5.8) as well as "The Bill of Rights: A Transcription" (Figure 5.9) both from the National Archives and Records Administration. Take a few minutes to read the texts. Then turn your attention to the tasks you could use to determine students' understanding of the texts and their ability to apply that knowledge in a variety of ways. Remember that this phase is focused on deep understanding and application. What is it that students should understand about these texts? There are any number of things that students could do with these texts, including investigations, presentations, discussions, and writing prompts. We encourage you to create your own so that students are inspired to take action after reading. If you'd like to check yourself, some questions that have been developed for these texts can be found on Corwin's companion website at www.corwin.com/textdependentquestions.

Figure 5.8   Excerpt From Introduction to *A More Perfect Union: The Creation of the United States Constitution* by Roger A. Bruns

The call for a bill of rights had been the anti-Federalists' most powerful weapon. Attacking the proposed Constitution for its vagueness and lack of specific protection against tyranny, Patrick Henry asked the Virginia convention, "What can avail your specious, imaginary balances, your rope-dancing, chain-rattling, ridiculous ideal checks and contrivances." The anti-Federalists, demanding a more concise, unequivocal Constitution, one that laid out for all to see the right of the people and limitations of the power of government, claimed that the brevity of the document only revealed its inferior nature. Richard Henry Lee despaired at the lack of provisions to protect "those essential rights of mankind without which liberty cannot exist." Trading the old government for the new without such a bill of rights, Lee argued, would be trading Scylla for Charybdis.

A bill of rights had been barely mentioned in the Philadelphia convention, most delegates holding that the fundamental rights of individuals had been secured in the state constitutions. James Wilson maintained that a bill of rights was superfluous because all power not expressly delegated to the new government was reserved to the people. It was clear, however, that in this argument the anti-Federalists held the upper hand. Even Thomas Jefferson, generally in favor of the new government, wrote to Madison that a bill of rights was "what the people are entitled to against every government on earth."

By the fall of 1788 Madison had been convinced that not only was a bill of rights necessary to ensure acceptance of the Constitution but that it would have positive effects. He wrote, on October 17, that such "fundamental maxims of free Government" would be "a good ground for an appeal to the sense of community" against potential oppression and would "counteract the impulses of interest and passion."

Madison's support of the bill of rights was of critical significance. One of the new representatives from Virginia to the First Federal Congress, as established by the new Constitution, he worked tirelessly to persuade the House to enact amendments. Defusing the anti-Federalists' objections to the Constitution, Madison was able to shepherd through 17 amendments in the early months of the Congress, a list that was later trimmed to 12 in the Senate. On October 2, 1789, President Washington sent to each of the states a copy of the 12 amendments adopted by the Congress in September. By December 15, 1791, three-fourths of the states had ratified the 10 amendments now so familiar to Americans as the "Bill of Rights."

Benjamin Franklin told a French correspondent in 1788 that the formation of the new government had been like a game of dice, with many players of diverse prejudices and interests unable to make any uncontested moves. Madison wrote to Jefferson that the welding of these clashing interests was "a task more difficult than can be well conceived by those who were not concerned in the execution of it." When the delegates left Philadelphia after the convention, few, if any, were convinced that the Constitution they had approved outlined the ideal form of government for the country. But late in his life James Madison scrawled out another letter, one never addressed. In it he declared that no government can be perfect, and "that which is the least imperfect is therefore the best government."

Source: Introduction by Roger A. Bruns to *A More Perfect Union: The Creation of the United States Constitution.* Washington, DC: Published for the National Archives and Records Administration by the National Archives Trust Fund Board, 1986.

Available for download from **www.corwin.com/textdependentquestions**

Figure 5.9 The Bill of Rights: A Transcription

The Preamble to the Bill of Rights

Congress of the United States begun and held at the City of New-York, on Wednesday the fourth of March, one thousand seven hundred and eighty nine.

THE Conventions of a number of the States, having at the time of their adopting the Constitution, expressed a desire, in order to prevent misconstruction or abuse of its powers, that further declaratory and restrictive clauses should be added: And as extending the ground of public confidence in the Government, will best ensure the beneficent ends of its institution.

RESOLVED by the Senate and House of Representatives of the United States of America, in Congress assembled, two thirds of both Houses concurring, that the following Articles be proposed to the Legislatures of the several States, as amendments to the Constitution of the United States, all, or any of which Articles, when ratified by three fourths of the said Legislatures, to be valid to all intents and purposes, as part of the said Constitution; viz.

ARTICLES in addition to, and Amendment of the Constitution of the United States of America, proposed by Congress, and ratified by the Legislatures of the several States, pursuant to the fifth Article of the original Constitution.

Note: The following text is a transcription of the first ten amendments to the Constitution in their original form. These amendments were ratified December 15, 1791, and form what is known as the "Bill of Rights."

Amendment I

Congress shall make no law respecting an establishment of religion, or prohibiting the free exercise thereof; or abridging the freedom of speech, or of the press; or the right of the people peaceably to assemble, and to petition the Government for a redress of grievances.

Amendment II

A well regulated Militia, being necessary to the security of a free State, the right of the people to keep and bear Arms, shall not be infringed.

Amendment III

No Soldier shall, in time of peace be quartered in any house, without the consent of the Owner, nor in time of war, but in a manner to be prescribed by law.

Amendment IV

The right of the people to be secure in their persons, houses, papers, and effects, against unreasonable searches and seizures, shall not be violated, and no Warrants shall issue, but upon

(Continued)

Figure 5.9   (Continued)

probable cause, supported by Oath or affirmation, and particularly describing the place to be searched, and the persons or things to be seized.

Amendment V

No person shall be held to answer for a capital, or otherwise infamous crime, unless on a presentment or indictment of a Grand Jury, except in cases arising in the land or naval forces, or in the Militia, when in actual service in time of War or public danger; nor shall any person be subject for the same offence to be twice put in jeopardy of life or limb; nor shall be compelled in any criminal case to be a witness against himself, nor be deprived of life, liberty, or property, without due process of law; nor shall private property be taken for public use, without just compensation.

Amendment VI

In all criminal prosecutions, the accused shall enjoy the right to a speedy and public trial, by an impartial jury of the State and district wherein the crime shall have been committed, which district shall have been previously ascertained by law, and to be informed of the nature and cause of the accusation; to be confronted with the witnesses against him; to have compulsory process for obtaining witnesses in his favor, and to have the Assistance of Counsel for his defence.

Amendment VII

In Suits at common law, where the value in controversy shall exceed twenty dollars, the right of trial by jury shall be preserved, and no fact tried by a jury, shall be otherwise re-examined in any Court of the United States, than according to the rules of the common law.

Amendment VIII

Excessive bail shall not be required, nor excessive fines imposed, nor cruel and unusual punishments inflicted.

Amendment IX

The enumeration in the Constitution, of certain rights, shall not be construed to deny or disparage others retained by the people.

Amendment X

The powers not delegated to the United States by the Constitution, nor prohibited by it to the States, are reserved to the States respectively, or to the people.

Available for download from **www.corwin.com/textdependentquestions**

Videos

To read a QR code, you must have a smartphone or tablet with a camera. We recommend that you download a QR code reader app that is made specifically for your phone or tablet brand.

Videos can also be accessed at
www.corwin.com/textdependentquestions

Video 5.1 Kindergarten students in Lisa Forehand's class finalize their discussion of *The Day the Crayons Quit.* Lisa models the structure of a letter from the narrator's point of view before the students practice writing their own.

Video 5.2 Alex Cabrera prompts his second grade students to write an expository essay on the effect supply and demand has on price, using textual evidence from the article they read about cow farmers.

Video 5.3 Shawna Codrington prompts her second grade students to use an opinion paragraph frame and textual evidence to write a paragraph explaining the most important moral of *Lon Po Po* before using iVideo to retell the folktale in their own words.

Video 5.4 Melissa Noble provides a writing prompt that asks her fourth grade students to compare the themes in two folktales, giving examples from each text to support their ideas.

CODA

We have spent a great deal of time discussing the role of text-dependent questions in helping students understand complex texts. We think that these questions are a critical scaffold for students to develop their understanding of the texts they read. We also think it's important that students learn to ask questions themselves. In fact, when students learn to ask these types of questions of their own reading, we know that they're prepared for their futures. In essence, the text-dependent questions that we ask should build students' habits, habits for inquiry and investigation that students can use across their academic careers. In fact, it's learning to ask and answer these types of questions, and to complete these types of tasks, that ensure that students are college- and career-ready.

APPENDICES

Questions for . . .

Appendix III: Grades 4–5

APPENDIX I
GRADES K-1

A·I

HI! FLY GUY BY TEDD ARNOLD

(NARRATIVE)

Questions for *Hi! Fly Guy* by Tedd Arnold

LEVEL 1

General Understanding

- What is this story about?
- What is the relationship between Buzz and Fly Guy?
- Is Fly Guy a good pet?

Key Details

- How do Buzz and the fly meet?
- What was Buzz looking for and why?
- How did the fly feel when he was put into the jar?
- Why did Buzz think that the fly was smart?
- Does the fly actually know the boy's name?
- How do Buzz's parents feel about his new pet?
- How does Buzz treat Fly Guy?
- Why did the judges change their minds?
- How did Fly Guy prove his intelligence to the judges?

LEVEL 2

Vocabulary

- What is the difference between a pet and a pest?
- Define *pest*.
- Where is an apostrophe used to form contractions in this book? Where is it used to show possession?

Structure

- What is dialogue? How is it used in this book? Read Buzz's and Fly Guy's lines aloud as you would expect them to speak the lines.
- Why are there three chapters in this book? Why does the author introduce new chapters in the book?
- The word *IS* is underlined on pages 13 and 27. Why?

Author's Craft

- Look at the illustrations on pages 4–5. What was Buzz prepared to catch?
- How did you know the boy's name before the author told you?
- Why do you think the author selected a fly to be the smartest pet in this story?

LEVEL 3

Author's Purpose

- Sometimes things aren't what they appear to be. In this case, the pest actually turned out to be a loyal and smart pet. Think about a time when something or someone wasn't what you had expected. Turn and tell your partner.

LEVEL 4

Opinion With Evidence or Argument

- How do you think Buzz felt in the part of the story on pages 18–19? What makes you say that?
- Which animal do you consider to be the smartest? Why? Draw a picture and write two to five sentences about why it is the smartest animal.
- Graph which pets students have in their houses. Write complete sentences about what the data show.

Available for download from **www.corwin.com/textdependentquestions**

PANCAKES FOR BREAKFAST
BY TOMIE DEPAOLA
(NARRATIVE)

Questions for *Pancakes for Breakfast* by Tomie DePaola

General Understanding

- What is this book about?
- How does the lady feel at the beginning, in the middle, and at the end of the book?
- Did she get what she wanted?

Key Details

- What does the lady want to make in the morning?
- How do the animals feel about her idea for breakfast? How do you know?
- What type of home does the lady have? Does she live in the city or the country? How do you know?
- Where does she get eggs and milk?
- Who gives her syrup?
- Reread the book, and focus on the animals. What do you notice the second time you read it?
- How did the lady's neighbors feel about her eating their pancakes? What tells you that they felt this way?

LEVEL 2

Vocabulary

- Does the lady follow the steps outlined in the recipe?
- What does the sign say at the end of the book?

Structure

- Do the illustrations follow or match the sequence of the recipe?
- Is the lady a good person in the end of the story or not? Why or why not?

Author's Craft

- How do the pictures tell the story?

LEVEL 3

Author's Purpose

- How do people feel when they make their own food?
- What does it mean to be *neighborly?*
- When have you had to try things several times? Did you succeed in the end or not? Why?

Intertextual Connections

- How is this book similar to or different from other books we have read that talk about helping other people?

LEVEL 4

Opinion With Evidence or Argument

- How did the author tell us, without using words, that the lady needed eggs?
- Is it easy to make pancakes? What in the text makes you say that?
- Draw a picture of when you helped someone. Write a paragraph about your picture.

Available for download from **www.corwin.com/textdependentquestions**

HOW PEOPLE LEARNED TO FLY
BY FRAN HODGKINS
(NONFICTION)

Questions for *How People Learned to Fly* by Fran Hodgkins

LEVEL 1

General Understanding
- What did people want to do?
- What does this book teach a reader?
- Why is flying important?

Key Details
- What does gravity do?
- What would happen if there were no gravity?
- How does the air impact us as we move?
- What can wind do?
- What did people attempt to do to be more like birds?
- Which wings worked best in order to fly? Why?
- What did having an engine allow people to do with their planes?

LEVEL 2

Vocabulary
- Who are Pegasus and Icarus?
- What is gravity?
- What are tiny air particles called?
- Explain drag. How are force and drag connected?
- What are gliders?
- Explain lift and how it works.
- What is an engine? How does one work?
- How do you create more lift?
- What is thrust? How do you create more thrust?

Structure

- What are apostrophes? How are they used in contractions in this book? What are other ways apostrophes are used in English?

Author's Craft

- The author uses birds a lot to explain the concept of flying and flight. How did humans' observation of birds influence their understanding of the concept of flight?

LEVEL 3

Author's Purpose

- What is the author teaching us as readers?
- Why is it important to study how people attempted different things in order to fly? What can a person learn from trying multiple times?

Intertextual Connections

- Create a chart or list of the content vocabulary in the book, and write your own definition for each word. Then draw a picture to represent the definition.
- Read a book about the Wright brothers or Charles Lindbergh. Compare their successful flight attempts with their unsuccessful ones. What made them famous? How did their decisions influence flight today?

LEVEL 4

Opinion With Evidence or Argument

- Create a summary of the book that includes at least three contractions.
- How are planes used today?
- What are the different purposes that planes serve?
- Are planes safe for the environment?
- Create a time line of inventions and attempts related to flight and flying.
- Conduct the paper airplane experiment in the back of the book. Log your attempts, and use the academic vocabulary from the book to explain what is happening when you attempt to fly your paper airplanes. What are the variables that you encounter that make flight successful or more of a challenge?

Available for download from **www.corwin.com/textdependentquestions**

TRUCK BY DONALD CREWS
(NONFICTION)

Questions for *Truck* by Donald Crews

LEVEL 1

General Understanding
- Why do we have big trucks?
- Does the truck take a long trip or a short journey?

Key Details
- What is this big truck carrying or moving from one place to the next?
- What types of weather does the truck encounter along its trip?
- Why does the truck have to stop?

LEVEL 2

Vocabulary
- What is written on the big red truck?
- What words do you see on other trucks?
- What do the signs tell the truck to do? How do you know?

Structure
- Describe the truck's trip. Where does it start, and where does it end? What were all of the stops and sights along the way?

Author's Craft
- How does the illustrator show us that the weather is changing along the trip?

LEVEL 3

Author's Purpose
- Why is it important to know about trucks?

LEVEL 4

Opinion With Evidence or Argument

- Where do you see trucks?

- What are the trucks moving from one place to the next? How do you know?

- How do trucks help people?

MY FIVE SENSES BY ALIKI
(SCIENCE)

Questions for *My Five Senses* by Aliki

LEVEL 1

General Understanding

- What is this book teaching us about?
- What are the five senses?
- What do we use for each of the senses?

Key Details

- What body part helps us see? Hear? Taste? Smell? Touch?
- What is the child in the book doing when he uses multiple senses? (For example, playing with the puppy requires seeing the puppy, listening to the puppy's sounds, smelling the puppy, and touching it while they play.)

LEVEL 2

Vocabulary

- Identify the verbs ending in *ing*.
- What does the word *tongue* mean?

Structure

- Study the use of the ellipses in the book. Did the author use them correctly? Why?
- Examine how the author uses different punctuation throughout the story. Read the text according to the punctuation being used.

Author's Craft

- How does the use of repetition influence our understanding?

LEVEL 3

Author's Purpose

- Why are the five senses important?
- What happens if we don't have a particular sense?

Intertextual Connections

- What is the role of guide dogs? How do guide dogs replace the sense of sight?
- Create a chart about your five senses similar to the one in the beginning of the book. Draw what you have seen, heard, tasted, smelled, and touched throughout the day. Was anything you sensed the same as what the child in the book sensed?

LEVEL 4

Opinion With Evidence or Argument

- Try moving around the room blindfolded, and then talk about how your other senses helped you compensate for the loss of sight.
- What are some activities that require the use of all five senses? Test your predictions. Graph the results on a chart. How many activities can you think of that require the use of all five senses?
- Which sense is the most important? Write a paragraph about why you feel this way. Which sense are you willing to not have? Write a paragraph about why you would choose to lose this sense. Create a graph comparing which sense your classmates feel is most important versus which is least important.

Available for download from **www.corwin.com/textdependentquestions**

STARFISH BY EDITH THACHER HURD
(SCIENCE)

Questions for *Starfish* by Edith Thacher Hurd

LEVEL 1

General Understanding
- What is this book about?
- What facts did you learn about starfish?
- Describe a starfish.
- Are all starfish the same?

Key Details
- Where do starfish live?
- How do starfish move?
- Explain how starfish eat.
- What happens when a starfish loses a ray?
- What body parts do starfish *not* have?
- How do starfish multiply?
- When do starfish multiply?

LEVEL 2

Vocabulary
- What are the starfish's arms called?
- What are tube feet? How do tube feet help starfish move in the water?
- Create a diagram and label the starfish parts.
- List different types of starfish and explain what makes them unique or special. How is each one different from the others?
- What are mussels, clams, and oysters?
- Describe how the baby starfish change and grow. Use vocabulary from the book.

Structure
- How does the author tell us when starfish have babies?
- Using the illustrations to help you, describe what is dangerous to starfish babies.

Author's Craft

- If a starfish has no hands, how does it "feel"?
- Why does the author say that the babies look like sand in the sea? Why is that important to think about in our heads? How does it help the babies?
- Why does the author talk so much about what baby starfish eat? Why do we need to know what they eat?

LEVEL 3

Author's Purpose

- What does this book teach us about starfish?
- How are starfish and humans similar or different?

Intertextual Connections

- Write two to three sentences comparing a starfish to another animal. You should consider their body parts, how they move, what they eat, and where they live. How are they similar or different?
- Research other animals that can lose a body part and grow it back. Why do you think they do this? How does this ability help the animal?
- [Depending on where you live] Where can we find starfish?
- Create the starfish as explained in the back of the book using those materials. Label your starfish and describe its lifecycle. Write a fictional or nonfiction story using your starfish as the main character. [The teacher can do this in a shared writing, or students can work independently.]

LEVEL 4

Opinion With Evidence or Argument

- Why is it important to learn about starfish?
- Are starfish protected? Should they be?
- How do starfish help maintain balance in the ocean?
- How are humans helping or harming starfish?

Available for download from **www.corwin.com/textdependentquestions**

APPENDIX II
GRADES 2-3

'BATS' BY RANDALL JARRELL
(POEM)

Questions for "Bats" by Randall Jarrell

General Understanding

- What is the subject of this poem?
- Describe what a newborn bat is like.

Key Details

- When do the mother and baby bat fly? When do the mother and baby bat sleep?
- Describe, using the author's words, how the mother flies. What does she do when she flies?
- What do bats eat?

Vocabulary

- How does the author describe the mother bat's cries?
- What words tell us what the bats look like?
- Does the mother bat like flying? How do you know?

Structure

- Does the poem begin at night or during the day? How do you know?
- Where does the poem begin? Where does it end? What does this tell us about a bat's life?

Author's Craft

- When the author says "shining needlepoints of sound," what is he talking about?
- The author says that the baby and mother bat's shadow is "printed on the moon." What does he mean by this?
- Does this poem rhyme? Why do you think the author chose not to use rhyming?

LEVEL 3

Author's Purpose

- How does the mother bat use her sense of sound?
- What does the mother bat do to care for her baby?

Intertextual Connections

- Think about how human mothers care for babies. What are the differences and similarities between how humans and bats care for their young?

LEVEL 4

Opinion With Evidence or Argument

- After reading this poem, write a paragraph on the following question:

  Do you think the bat from the poem is a good mother? Why or why not?

Available for download from **www.corwin.com/textdependentquestions**

THE RAFT BY JIM LAMARCHE
(NARRATIVE)

Questions for *The Raft* by Jim LaMarche

LEVEL 1

General Understanding

- How does Nicky feel about spending the summer with his grandma at the beginning of the story?
- Compare how Nicky feels at the beginning of the story versus the end.
- How does Nicky pass the time while staying with his grandma?
- What happens in the story?

Key Details

- Why does Nicky need to spend the summer with his grandma?
- Where does his grandma live?
- Describe his grandma's house.
- Why does Nicky not do what his grandma suggests in the beginning of the story?
- Which animals and wildlife appear throughout the story?
- Nicky's grandma was not surprised by the raft. Why is this?
- What has his grandma been waiting to give to Nicky?
- What happens to the doe and fawn? How does Nicky help?

LEVEL 2

Vocabulary

- Define *river rat.* Who are the river rats in the story? Why?
- Describe how you "pole down a river."
- What are cattails? How do the illustrations help you understand what these are?
- Nicky describes the drawings as "wild, fast and free." What does that mean?
- Nicky's grandma says that she and her friends were a "herd of wild animals." What does this mean? What does this tell us about his grandma's personality and childhood?

Structure

- Is there a connection between the animals that are drawn on the raft and the animals that Nicky encounters throughout the story?

Author's Craft

- What role do the animals play throughout the story?
- Which animal interaction had the biggest impact or influence on Nicky? Why do you think this?
- Nicky says, "Somehow, on the river, it seemed like summer would never end. But of course it did." How does the author help us feel like summer is endless for Nicky?

LEVEL 3

Author's Purpose

- What does Jim LaMarche want boys and girls to think about after reading this story?
- What does the raft represent to Nicky? To his grandma?
- Who do you think drew the animals on the raft? Why?
- Who do you think the raft belongs to? Why?

Intertextual Connections

- Why did Jim LaMarche write a note from the author at the beginning of the book? How is his note similar to and/or different from the story he wrote?

LEVEL 4

Opinion With Evidence or Argument

- What is Nicky's relationship like with his grandma? How does it change and develop over the course of the story?
- What did Nicky learn during his summer with his grandma?
- What is symbolic about Nicky drawing the deer on the raft? Why does his grandma want to make it permanent?

Available for download from **www.corwin.com/textdependentquestions**

THE SIGN PAINTER BY ALLEN SAY
(FICTIONAL NARRATIVE)

Questions for *The Sign Painter* by Allen Say

LEVEL 1

General Understanding

- Why does the young boy pass through the town?
- Do the sign painter and the young boy get along? Describe their relationship.
- Who is the man in the white suit?

Key Details

- Where does this story take place? (Use the pictures and the car to help you.)
- Why do the sing painter and the young boy start working together?
- Does the young boy consider himself to be an artist? Do you agree or disagree? Why?
- Do you think that the young boy and the sign painter would make a good team, as he says on page 14? Why or why not?
- Is the man in the white suit a dreamer? Why or why not?
- On page 30, the man asks the young boy if the man in the white suit will succeed, and the young boy says that he hopes so. What are they talking about?

LEVEL 2

Vocabulary

- What is a billboard? Where do you see them?
- What is a canvas? What types of surfaces can be used as a canvas?
- Why is the sign painter flushed after receiving the job for 12 billboards?
- What does being a "wage earner" mean?
- What is the mesa that the author refers to on page 24?
- What is the curtain that the author refers to on page 26?

Structure

- Why is the young boy described the way he is at the beginning of the story? What does this tell the reader?
- Explain why the author uses an ellipsis on page 28. What does the ellipsis tell the reader?
- How does the author use punctuation to create mood and/or tone within the text?

Author's Craft

- How does the author describe the envelope being handed to the sign painter? How does this make you feel? Why?
- The author leaves out many details, such as who certain characters are and what things mean, and he provides only portions of conversations. Why does he do this?
- What do the billboards represent?
- Are dreams like clouds? (refer to page 30)

LEVEL 3

Author's Purpose

- What is the author's message?
- Do the characters follow their dreams? Who does and who doesn't?
- Why is the young boy alone?
- What is the role of the sign painter? Why doesn't he question the job that has been given to him? What does this say about him as a person?
- Does the sign painter follow his dream? Why or why not?
- The houses are empty. What does this mean?
- What is the meaning behind the word *Arrowstar*?

Intertextual Connections

- Talk to a partner about your dreams. Have you ever attempted to achieve one of your dreams? What did you do to achieve your dream? Are you still trying to achieve your dream? What obstacles have you encountered along the way? Who has supported you? Share what your partner said with your table or class.

LEVEL 4

Opinion With Evidence or Argument

- On page 14, the man asks the boy, "How does it feel to be a wage earner?" The boy replies with, "I am a painter." In turn the man says, "We all have dreams." Throughout the book, what is the significance of dreams and following one's dreams? Who follows their dreams? Who doesn't? What symbolizes a dream in the story?
- Research some people in your family, school, or community. Write a one-page paper about whether or not they have followed their dream(s). What made them successful? What challenges did they encounter? Do they continue to dream and strive to achieve their dreams?

MARTIN LUTHER KING JR. AND THE MARCH ON WASHINGTON BY FRANCES E. RUFFIN

(HISTORY/NONFICTION)

Questions for *Martin Luther King Jr. and the March on Washington* by Frances E. Ruffin

LEVEL 1

General Understanding

- What event is taking place in this story?
- Where does this story take place?
- When does this story take place?

Key Details

- Where have the people listening to Dr. King come from?
- Why is Dr. King giving his speech?
- Why do A. Philip Randolph and Bayard Rustin choose Washington, DC, as the protest site?

LEVEL 2

Vocabulary

- What does *segregation* mean?
- What are civil rights?
- What is a protest?

Structure

- Look at the photographs of the facilities for white people and those for colored people. Do they look the same? Why or why not?
- Examine the pictures in the book. Are they all the same? Which tell the story better—the drawings or the photographs?

Author's Craft

- What laws in the South does the author tell us about? Why does she do this?
- How does the author describe Martin Luther King Jr.?
- How does the author show Dr. King's speech was effective?

LEVEL 3

Author's Purpose

- Is Martin Luther King Jr. important to the people in the story? How do you know?
- Why did Dr. King give his speech at the Lincoln Memorial?
- Is protesting easy? What happens to some people when they protest?
- Are "regular" people the only ones watching the speech? Why is this important?

Intertextual Connections

- Review the final picture in the book. How does this help you to understand the importance of Dr. King's speech?
- Watch a clip of the "I Have a Dream" speech. Does the video support the ideas presented in the book? Did you like the video or the book better? Why?

LEVEL 4

Opinion With Evidence or Argument

- Think about our society today compared to the time Dr. King lived in. How are they different? How are they the same? What has changed because of his speech?

Available for download from **www.corwin.com/textdependentquestions**

SO YOU WANT TO BE PRESIDENT?
BY JUDITH ST. GEORGE

(HISTORY/NONFICTION)

Questions for *So You Want to Be President?* by Judith St. George

LEVEL 1

General Understanding

- What is the subject of the book?

Key Details

- What are the good things about being president?
- What are the bad things about being president?
- What is the most popular name among presidents?
- How old does a person have to be to become president?
- Name some of the pets our presidents have had.
- Who hasn't become president yet?

LEVEL 2

Vocabulary

- What do you think an adversary is?
- Explain what a brawl is.
- What did Lincoln mean when he said "If I am two-faced, would I wear the one I have now"? How does this reveal his personality?
- What is a ditty?
- Explain what an assassination is.

Structure

- How do the quotations from people who knew the presidents help you understand the presidents' personalities better?
- How does the picture on pages 40 and 41 help you understand what *impeached* means?

Author's Craft

- What comparisons does the author make among the different presidents (their looks, whether they liked being president, pets, etc.)? What does this tell us about the role of president and who can fill it?

- Why does the author choose to include the negative personality traits of our past presidents?

LEVEL 3

Author's Purpose

- Describe the differences among some of the presidents with respect to how they looked, acted, and felt about the presidency.

- How does the author feel about presidents? How do you know?

- What do "good" presidents do?

Intertextual Connections

- Review the oath that presidents have to take. What does it mean to you? Based on what you read in the book, have the presidents mentioned done what they swore they would do in the oath?

LEVEL 4

Opinion With Evidence or Argument

- Look at the list of presidents in the back of this book. Choose one and research him. In a short paragraph, explain whether or not you think your chosen president is/was a "good" one.

Available for download from **www.corwin.com/textdependentquestions**

A DROP OF WATER BY WALTER WICK
(SCIENCE/NONFICTION)

Questions for *A Drop of Water* by Walter Wick

LEVEL 1

General Understanding
- What is the subject of the book?
- What are the different phases of water discussed in this book?

Key Details
- What are particles?
- When the molecules in water start moving more slowly, what does it become?
- When heat is introduced to water, what happens to the molecules?
- How does attraction relate to water molecules?

LEVEL 2

Vocabulary
- What is a molecule?
- Define sphere.
- Why are water molecules able to cling together, even when falling?
- Define surface tension.
- Describe capillary attraction.
- Explain the difference between evaporation and condensation.
- How are sleet and snowflakes different? Why?
- Define refraction.
- Give an example of a type of wavelength.

Structure
- How do the pictures (like the pin on page 7) help you understand how water works?
- How does the picture on page 13 illustrate capillary attraction?
- How does each section of the book build upon the others? Could you fully understand the end section (The Water Cycle) without knowing about surface tension or how water interacts with heat? Why or why not?

Author's Craft

- Would you call this book a story? Why or why not?
- What comparison does the author make to help us understand the surface tension that makes water molecules cling together?
- What examples does the author use to describe surface tension?
- How does the example of the pin floating in water help you understand surface tension and how it works?

LEVEL 3

Author's Purpose

- Why do you think the author wrote this book?
- What do the examples of the pin, egg, water tubes, and bubble illustrate about water's properties?
- How do clouds and snowflakes relate to what you learned about surface tension in the beginning of the book?
- Examine the pictures used to illustrate the properties of water in the book. Why do you think the author chose these examples? Why do you think he chose pictures instead of drawings?

Intertextual Connections

- How does the epigraph at the beginning of the book explain the main ideas of the text?
- Imagine this book without pictures. How would the information change?

LEVEL 4

Opinion With Evidence or Argument

- How is water important in our everyday lives? Create an argumentative speech in which you describe the importance of water in our everyday lives. Be sure to include specific details from the book that show how water is an integral part of our planet.

FROM SEEDS TO PLANT
BY GAIL GIBBONS
(SCIENCE/NONFICTION)

Questions for *From Seeds to Plant* by Gail Gibbons

LEVEL 1

General Understanding

- What is this story about?
- Name the different types of plants you see in the story.

Key Details

- How does a seed get food?
- What must happen for a seed to sprout and grow into a plant?

LEVEL 2

Vocabulary

- What is nectar?
- Describe how a pod helps seeds grow.
- Describe the parts that make up a flower.
- Name the parts of a seed.
- What is germination?

Structure

- How do the diagrams in this book help us understand the structure of seeds and flowers?

Author's Craft

- How do the labels on the pictures help you understand how seeds and flowers work?
- Would you call this book a story? Why or why not?

LEVEL 3

Author's Purpose

- Do all seeds look the same? Why or why not?
- What is pollination, and how does it happen?

- What role do animals play in the development of seeds into plants?
- Compare the different ways pods and seeds can be transported.
- Why are buds important?
- What do you think the author's main purpose for writing this book was?

Intertextual Connections

- Compare the pictures of the seeds with the pictures of the plants they eventually grow into. Are they the same? How are they different?
- Read the project "From a Seed to a Plant." How do you see the life cycle of a seed and plant taking place in this project?
- The last page of the book gives additional information on plants. Do any of the facts here remind you of facts you learned from the main part of the book?

LEVEL 4

Opinion With Evidence or Argument

- Write a short story from the perspective of a seed. Begin with your life inside a flower. Be sure to include details from the book to support the different parts of your transformation into a plant.

Available for download from **www.corwin.com/textdependentquestions**

APPENDIX III
GRADES 4-5

'MY SHADOW'
BY ROBERT LOUIS STEVENSON
(POEM)

Questions for "My Shadow" by Robert Louis Stevenson

LEVEL 1

General Understanding

- What is the subject of this poem?
- Is the narrator a boy or a girl? How do you know?

Key Details

- When does the shadow appear?
- What is the "funniest" thing about the shadow?
- What happens to the shadow in the last stanza?

LEVEL 2

Vocabulary

- Describe what the shadow looks like. Is it always the same?
- What is a notion?
- The narrator says the shadow is not like "proper children." What does *proper* mean?

Structure

- Does this poem rhyme? How does this affect the tone of the text?

Author's Craft

- What does the narrator call his shadow?
- When the shadow is described and shooting "up taller like an india-rubber ball" and getting "so little that there's none of him," what's actually happening?

LEVEL 3

Author's Purpose

- How does the narrator feel about his shadow? How do you know?
- Does the narrator think of this shadow as being a part of himself? Why or why not?

Intertextual Connections

- Think about your own shadow. Does it do some of the same things the shadow in the poem does? Which ones?

LEVEL 4

Opinion With Evidence or Argument

- The narrator says of his shadow: "What can be the use of him is more than I can see." Do you think he actually thinks shadows are useless? In a short paragraph, explain whether or not you think the narrator likes his shadow.

Available for download from **www.corwin.com/textdependentquestions**

THE SECRET GARDEN
BY FRANCES HODGSON BURNETT
(CHAPTER 1)
(NOVEL)

Please note this text is widely available online to print and distribute in class.

Questions for *The Secret Garden* by Frances Hodgson Burnett (Chapter 1)

General Understanding

- Who is the main character in this text? Describe her home life.
- Where does this story take place?
- What sickness is breaking out among her household?

Key Details

- Who is Mem Sahib? What do you think this means?
- What is Mary's mother like?
- Explain the effect cholera has had on the people in Mary's community.
- How does Mary survive the cholera outbreak?

Vocabulary

- Mary is described as being "cross." What does this word mean in the story?
- What is an *Ayah*? How do you know?
- How is Mary's personality described? What words, specifically, does the author use to paint a picture of her as a character?

Structure

- At what point in time does this story take place: after the cholera outbreak, or before?
- What information does the narrator include about Mary at the beginning of the story? Why?
- When does Mary discover that cholera has killed everyone in her home?

Author's Craft

- What actions of Mary's support the narrator's idea that she was "as tyrannical and selfish a pig as ever lived"?

- Explain how the author uses irony in Mary's interaction with the snake.

- Describe the social classes that live in Mary's household. Use specific evidence to support your thinking.

LEVEL 3

Author's Purpose

- Does Mary love her Ayah? What does this tell us about her and her family?

- What does the narrator mean when he or she says, "When people had cholera it seemed they remembered nothing but themselves"? Does Mary believe anyone will come for her?

Intertextual Connections

- Read Rudyard Kipling's poem "Cholera Camp." Compare and contrast how the excerpt from *The Secret Garden* and the poem describe a cholera outbreak.

LEVEL 4

Opinion With Evidence or Argument

- After reading this excerpt, write a short analysis of Mary as a character. What personality traits does she exhibit? Why? Be sure to use the way she was treated as a child to support your ideas and conclusions.

WE ARE THE SHIP: THE STORY OF THE NEGRO LEAGUE BASEBALL BY KADIR NELSON ("1ST INNING")
(HISTORY/NONFICTION)

Questions for *We Are the Ship: The Story of the Negro League Baseball* by Kadir Nelson ("1st Inning")

General Understanding
- What is the subject of the book?
- What group of people, specifically, is this book about?

Key Details
- Before the 1860s, who were the only people who played baseball?
- How were African Americans playing baseball treated at this time?
- Why did African American players start to disappear from baseball by the late 1800s?
- What inspired African American players to start their own teams?
- Who is Rube Foster?
- What was the name of Foster's team?

LEVEL 2

Vocabulary
- How does the author explain the origins of the words *Negro* and *colored*?
- What does the author mean when he says, "It just gave them a little more ambition to slide feet first when a Negro was covering the base"? What does this reveal about how the African American players were treated?
- What is a "gentleman's agreement"? Do you think this is appropriate wording, given what the phrase means?

Structure
- How does the epigraph at the beginning of the book connect to the main ideas of the text?
- How do the quotations at the beginning of this section of the story help you to understand it better?

- Why did the author choose to include drawings of the players he mentions? What does this add to the story being told?

Author's Craft

- How does the author describe Rube Foster's personality? How does this help us understand what was needed to start an all-Negro league?

- Consider the author's "voice." How would you describe it? Why? Point to specific parts of the text that inform your thinking.

LEVEL 3

Author's Purpose

- What is the author's relationship to the Negro baseball leagues? How do you know?

- What was different about how Rube Foster approached his baseball teams?

- Was it important that the teams Foster put together had clean, well-maintained equipment? Why or why not?

- When describing Foster, the author says, "He gave black baseball dignity and set the standard for things to come." What does this mean? How do you think this affected later leagues for African Americans?

Intertextual Connections

- Read the foreword to the story. How does Hank Aaron's experience connect to the experiences of the other players mentioned in the story?

- Look at the drawing of the first World Series. Do the players match the descriptions you read about? How does this drawing change what you know about the leagues so far? Is anything different from what you expected?

LEVEL 4

Opinion With Evidence or Argument

- In a short paragraph, assess Rube Foster's leadership for the first all-Negro baseball teams. Do you think he did an effective job setting the stage for later leagues? Why or why not?

Available for download from **www.corwin.com/textdependentquestions**

ABOUT TIME BY BRUCE KOSCIELNIAK
(HISTORY/SCIENCE/NONFICTION)

Questions for *About Time* by Bruce Koscielniak

LEVEL 1

General Understanding

- Why is time important?
- What is the author teaching us about time?
- How has telling time changed over the course of history?

Key Details

- How is time measured?
- How was time measured in the past versus the present?
- Why was seasonal time so important to know and track?
- How many days are there in a year? (notice the ¼)
- How were calendars developed?
- What happens in one year?
- Why was daylight saving time originally put into use?
- Are measurements of time accurate?
- Explain how different time zones were created and why.

LEVEL 2

Vocabulary

- Explain the evolution of the week.
- What is a leap year?
- What is the Gregorian calendar, and who uses it?
- What is an obelisk?
- Explain how a clepsydra worked.
- What is the science of timekeeping called?
- How can a second be broken into parts?

Structure

- How do the illustrations and diagrams help enhance or clarify your understanding of the text?

Author's Craft

- How does the author organize the book and its information?
- Where does the author use humor or play on words? Is it effective for you as a reader?

LEVEL 3

Author's Purpose

- As clock making became more sophisticated and precise, what happened to the economy? Why?

Intertextual Connections

- Compare the invention of the clock to other inventions you have studied in school. Which invention is most important? Why? Use evidence from the texts to support your claims.
- Read Einstein's theory of relativity. How does it relate to time?

LEVEL 4

Opinion With Evidence or Argument

- Create a time line that explains the documentation of time. How does it develop and change over the course of the time line?
- Research ancient ways of telling time. Which ones were the most effective, and which were least effective?
- Write an argumentative paper on the pros and cons of daylight saving time. Should the United States still implement it?
- Is time cyclical? Defend your answer in an essay.

Available for download from **www.corwin.com/textdependentquestions**

'THE SLINKY' BY DON WULFFSON FROM *TOYS! AMAZING STORIES BEHIND SOME GREAT INVENTIONS* (PAGES 5-10)

(NONFICTION)

Questions for "The Slinky" by Don Wulffson From *Toys! Amazing Stories Behind Some Great Inventions* (pages 5–10)

LEVEL 1

General Understanding

- What type of text is this? How do you know?
- What is the Slinky?
- What is a spring?
- How was the Slinky invented?

Key Details

- Who invented the Slinky?
- What was Richard James trying to invent?
- Why did the navy want something to counterbalance the instruments?
- How does a spring function?
- Was Richard James successful according to the navy? Why or why not?
- How did Richard James "discover" the Slinky?
- How were Richard James's views and Betty James's views of the purpose of the Slinky different?
- How did the Jameses market the Slinky?
- Describe the sales of the Slinky.

LEVEL 2

Vocabulary

- Using vocabulary from the second paragraph, describe what is happening to a ship when it is unstable.
- What does *counterbalance* mean?
- Explain what *toiled* means in the sentence, "For weeks he *toiled*, making dozens of different devices."
- Define the word *slinky*.

Structure

- How does the author use punctuation to create suspense or excitement in this piece?
- Explain the passage of time in the piece. How does it influence the reader's understanding of the invention of the Slinky?

Author's Craft

- Explain the function of the bulleted list at the end of the text.
- Does the author use words or punctuation to create the tone?

LEVEL 3

Author's Purpose

- What is the purpose of writing a story about the Slinky?
- How does understanding where the Slinky originated influence how you view the toy today?

Intertextual Connections

- Compare the invention of the Slinky to the invention of another toy described in the book. Can you find a toy that was used for another purpose than what it was originally intended for?

LEVEL 4

Opinion With Evidence or Argument

- Research the distribution, marketing, and profit of the Slinky for the past 50-plus years.
  - Do you agree or disagree with how the Slinky has been produced?
  - Given the information in the text combined with your own research, what would you have done the same or differently?

'WORDS AS FREE AS CONFETTI' BY PAT MORA

(POEM)

Questions for "Words as Free as Confetti" by Pat Mora

General Understanding

- What type of text is this? How do you know?
- What is the topic of this poem?

Key Details

- Which senses does the author write about in this poem?

Vocabulary

- What is the tone of the piece? How do we know? Point out specific words or phrases.
- Find the words in italics—what do the italics indicate? What are *gatitos*? What is an *abuelita*?
- What does *yo soy libre* mean?

Structure

- What is the rhyme scheme of the poem? Why do you think the author made this choice?
- What is the title of the poem? What is confetti? How does the idea of "confetti" reappear in the lines of the poem?

Author's Craft

- Find a simile in the poem. How does the author use similes to make her poem more vivid?
- How does the use of both English and Spanish in the poem change its meaning?
- Mora uses words like *searoar* and *chestnutwind*. What do you think these mean? How do they support her ideas about the power of words?
- Where does the author use repetition? What effect does it have on the message of the poem?

LEVEL 3

Author's Purpose

- Does the author think of words as a good or bad thing? How do you know? Use specific lines from the poem to inform your thinking.

- In the first few lines of the poem, Mora says she can taste words "sweet as plump plums,/ bitter as old lemons." Where else does she use this type of sensory language, and with which senses? What do you think she is trying to say about words?

- Mora refers to words as "you." Why does she do this? How does it change how you think of words?

Intertextual Connections

- Imagine this poem without the use of Spanish words and phrases. How would the meaning of the poem change? Why?

LEVEL 4

Opinion With Evidence or Argument

- Do you think words can set you free, as Mora suggests in the poem? Using evidence from this text, as well as your own personal experience, write an argument for or against the power of words. Do they really have the ability to do everything Mora says they do? Be sure to support your claims with specific details.

Available for download from **www.corwin.com/textdependentquestions**

REFERENCES

Adams, M. J. (1990). *Beginning to read: Thinking and learning about print*. Cambridge, MA: MIT Press.

Adler, M. J., & Van Doren, C. (1972). *How to read a book*. New York, NY: Touchstone. (Original work published 1940)

Baumann, J. F., Kame'enui, E. J., & Ash, G. E. (2003). Research on vocabulary instruction: Voltaire redux. In J. Flood, D. Lapp, J. R. Squire, & J. M. Jensen (Eds.), *Handbook of research on teaching the English language arts* (2nd ed., pp. 752–785). Mahwah, NJ: Erlbaum.

Beck, I. L., & McKeown, M. G. (2001). Text talk: Capturing the benefits of read-aloud experiences with young children. *The Reading Teacher, 55*(1), 10–20.

Beck, I. L., McKeown, M. G., Hamilton, R. L., & Kucan, L. (1997). *Questioning the author: An approach for enhancing student engagement with text*. Newark, NJ: International Reading Association.

Billings, L., & Fitzgerald, J. (2002). Dialogic discussion and the paideia seminar. *American Educational Research Journal, 39*(4), 907–941.

Boyles, N. (2013). Closing in on close reading. *Educational Leadership, 70*(4), 36–41.

Bransford, J. D., Brown, A. L., & Cocking, R. R. (Eds.). (2000). *How people learn: Brain, mind, experience, and school*. Committee on Developments in the Science of Learning and Committee on Learning Research and Educational Practice. Washington, DC: National Academy Press.

Britton, J. (1983). Writing and the story of the world. In B. Kroll & E. Wells (Eds.), *Explorations in the development of writing theory, research, and practice* (pp. 3–30). New York, NY: Wiley.

Brown, M. W. (1949). *The important book*. New York, NY: Harper & Row.

Brown, S., & Kappes, L. (2012). *Implementing the Common Core State Standards: A primer on "close reading of text."* Washington, DC: The Aspen Institute.

Callender, A. A., & McDaniel, M. A. (2007). The benefits of embedded question adjuncts for low and high structure builders. *Journal of Educational Psychology, 99*(2), 339–348.

Castek, J., & Beach, R. (2013). Using apps to support disciplinary literacy and science learning. *Journal of Adolescent & Adult Literacy, 56*(7), 554–564.

Chi, M. T. H., & Bassock, M. (1989). Learning from examples via self-explanation. In L. Resnick (Ed.), *Knowing, learning and instruction: Essays in honour of Robert Glaser* (pp. 251–282). Hillsdale, NJ: Erlbaum.

Collins, S. (2010). *The hunger games*. New York, NY: Scholastic.

Common Core State Standards Initiative (CCSSI). (2010a). *Common Core State Standards for English language arts & literacy in history/social studies, science, and technical subjects*. Retrieved from http://www.corestandards.org/ELA-Literacy

Common Core State Standards Initiative (CCSSI). (2010b). *Common Core State Standards for mathematical practice.* Retrieved from http://www.corestandards.org/math

Covey, S. R. (2004). *The seven habits of highly effective people.* New York, NY: Simon & Schuster.

Cromley, J., Perez, T., Fitzhugh, S., Newcombe, N., Wills, T., & Tanaka, J. (2013). Improving students' diagram comprehension with classroom instruction. *Journal of Experimental Education, 81*(4), 511–537.

Daniels, H., & Harvey, S. (2009). *Comprehension and collaboration: Inquiry circles in action.* Portsmouth, NH: Heinemann.

Daywalt, D. (2013). *The day the crayons quit.* New York, NY: Penguin.

de Saint-Exupéry, A. (1943/2000). *The little prince.* New York, NY: Mariner.

DiCamillo, K. (2013). *Flora and Ulysses.* Somerville, MA: Candlewick Press.

Edwards, R. E. (2008). *Competitive debate: The official guide.* New York, NY: Penguin.

Eeds, M., & Wells, D. (1989). Grand conversations: An exploration of meaning construction in literature study groups. *Research in the Teaching of English, 23*(1), 4–29.

Eisner, E. W. (1991). *The enlightened eye: Qualitative inquiry and the enhancement of educational practice.* New York, NY: Macmillan.

Fisher, D., & Frey, N. (2012). Close reading in elementary schools. *The Reading Teacher, 66,* 179–188.

Fisher, D., & Frey, N. (2014a). *Better learning through structured teaching: A framework for the gradual release of responsibility* (2nd ed.). Alexandria, VA: ASCD.

Fisher, D., & Frey, N. (2014b). Scaffolded reading instruction of complex texts. *The Reading Teacher, 67*(5), 347–352.

Freedman, R. (1987). *Lincoln: A photobiography.* New York: Clarion Books.

Frey, N., & Fisher, D. (2009). *Learning words inside and out: Vocabulary instruction that boosts achievement in all subject areas grades 1–6.* Portsmouth, NH: Heinemann.

Frey, N., Fisher, D., & Gonzalez, A. (2010). *Literacy 2.0: Reading and writing in 21st century classrooms.* Bloomington, IN: Solution Tree.

Gallagher, K. (2011). *Write like this: Teaching real-world writing through modeling and mentor texts.* Portland, ME: Stenhouse.

Gallaz, C., & Innocenti, R. (1985). *Rose Blanche.* Mankato, MN: Creative Editions.

Gernsbacher, M. (1991). Cognitive processes and mechanisms in language comprehension: The structure building framework. *Psychology of Learning & Motivation, 27,* 217–263.

Haeffner, C. (2006). Cool speeches! *School Library Monthly, 23*(2), 22–23.

Halliday, M. A. K. (1977). *Learning how to mean: Explorations in the development of language.* New York, NY: Elsevier.

Hansen, J. (2001). *When writers read* (2nd ed.). Portsmouth, NH: Heinemann.

Henkes, K. (1991). *Chrysanthemum.* New York, NY: Mulberry.

Hesse, K. (1996). *The music of dolphins.* New York, NY: Scholastic.

Hesse, K. (1997). *Out of the dust.* New York, NY: Scholastic.

Hillary, E. (2000). *View from the summit: The remarkable memoir from the first person to conquer Everest.* New York, NY: Gallery.

Hoose, P., & Hoose, H. (1998). *Hey, little ant.* Berkeley, CA: Tricycle Press.

Kurland, D. J. (1995). *I know what it says . . . what does it mean? Critical skills for critical reading.* Belmont, CA: Wadsworth.

Lally, P., van Jaarsveld, C. H. M., Potts, H. W. W., & Wardle, J. (2010). How are habits formed: Modeling habit formation in the real world. *European Journal of Social Psychology, 40*(6), 998–1009.

Lasky, K. (1997). *Marven of the great north woods.* Clermont, FL: Paw Prints.

Marzano, R., Pickering, D., & Heflebower, T. (2011). *The highly engaged classroom.* Bloomington, IN: Marzano Research Laboratory.

Mason, J. M., Stahl, S. A., Au, K. H., & Herman, P. A. (2003). Reading: Children's developing knowledge of words. In J. Flood, D. Lapp, J. R. Squire, & J. M. Jensen (Eds.), *Handbook of research on teaching the English language arts* (2nd ed., pp. 914–930). Mahwah, NJ: Erlbaum.

McLaughlin, M., & DeVoogd, G. (2004). *Critical literacy: Enhancing students' reading comprehension.* New York, NY: Scholastic.

Mezuk, B., Bondarenko, I., Smith, S., & Tucker, E. (2011). The influence of a policy debate program on high school achievement in a large urban public school system. *Educational Research and Reviews, 6*(9), 622–635.

Milne, A. A. (1926). *Winnie-the-pooh.* New York, NY: Dutton.

Newkirk, T. (2012). *The art of slow reading.* Portsmouth, NH: Heinemann.

Newman, P. (2014). *Plastic ahoy! Investigating the great Pacific garbage patch.* Minneapolis, MN: Millbrook Press.

Nichols, W. D., Rupley, W. H., & Rasinski, T. (2009). Fluency in learning to read for meaning: Going beyond repeated readings. *Literacy Research and Instruction, 48*(1), 1–13.

Norgay, T., & Ullman, J. R. (1955, May 9). Tenzing: The tiger of Everest. *Sports Illustrated, 2*(19), 37–49. Retrieved from http://sportsillustrated.cnn.com/vault/edb/reader.html?magID=SI&issueDate=19550509&mode=reader_vault

Nystrand, M. (2006). Research on the role of classroom discourse as it affects reading comprehension. *Research in the Teaching of English, 40*(4), 392–412.

Peverly, S. T., & Wood, R. (2001). The effects of adjunct questions and feedback on improving the reading comprehension skills of learning-disabled adolescents. *Contemporary Educational Psychology, 26*(1), 25–43.

Pfaffinger, K. (2006). Research paper baby steps. *English Journal, 95*(4), 75–77.

Prelutsky, J. (1983). *The Random House book of poetry for children.* New York, NY: Random House.

Reznitskaya, A. (2012). Dialogic teaching: Rethinking language use during literature discussions. *The Reading Teacher, 65*(7), 446–456.

Roberts, T., & Billings, L. (2012). *Teaching critical thinking: Using seminars for 21st century literacy.* Larchmont, NY: Eye on Education.

Ryan, P. M. (1999). *Riding freedom.* New York, NY: Scholastic.

Shannon, D. (1998a). *A bad case of stripes.* New York, NY: Blue Sky Press.

Shannon, D. (1998b). *No, David!* New York, NY: Blue Sky Press.

Simon, S. (1993). *Weather.* New York, NY: HarperCollins.

Simon, S. (1997). *The brain: Our nervous system.* New York, NY: HarperCollins.

Thayer, E. L. (2000). *Ernest L. Thayer's Casey at the bat: A ballad of the Republic sung in the year 1888 / copiously and faithfully illustrated by Christopher Bing.* Brooklyn, NY: Handprint Books. (Original work published 1888)

Therrien, W. J. (2004). Fluency and comprehension gains as a result of repeated reading: A meta-analysis. *Remedial & Special Education, 25*(4), 252–261.

Trueman, T. (2000). *Stuck in neutral.* New York, NY: HarperCollins Publishers.

Wallechinsky, I., Wallace, D., & Wallace, A. (1977). *The book of lists.* New York, NY: William Morrow.

Webb, N. L. (2002). *Alignment study in language arts, mathematics, science, and social studies of state standards and assessments for four states.* Washington, DC: Council of Chief State School Officers.

White, T. G., Graves, M. F., & Slater, W. H. (1990). Growth of reading vocabulary in diverse elementary schools: Decoding and word meaning. *Journal of Educational Psychology, 82,* 281–290.

Wilkerson, I. A. G., & Son, E. H. (2011). A dialogic turn in research on learning and teaching to comprehend. In M. L. Kamil, P. D. Pearson, E. B. Moje, & P. P. Afflerbach (Eds.), *Handbook of reading research* (Vol. IV, pp. 359–387). New York, NY: Routledge.

Wineburg, S., Martin, D., & Monte-Sano, C. (2011). *Reading like a historian: Teaching literacy in middle and high school history classrooms.* New York, NY: Teachers College Press.

Yolen, J. (1992). *Encounter.* San Diego, CA: Harcourt Brace.

Zusak, M. (2005). *The book thief.* Sydney, NSW, Australia: Picador.

Zywica, J., & Gomez, K. (2008). Annotating to support learning in the content areas: Teaching and learning science. *Journal of Adolescent & Adult Literacy, 52*(2), 155–165.

INDEX

ABOUT THE AUTHORS

 **Douglas Fisher, PhD**, is professor of educational leadership at San Diego State University and a teacher-leader at Health Sciences High & Middle College. He is the recipient of an IRA Celebrate Literacy Award, the NCTE's Farmer Award for Excellence in Writing, and a Christa McAuliffe Award for Excellence in Teacher Education. A former board member for the Literacy Research Association and a current board member for the International Reading Association, Doug is also a credentialed English teacher and administrator in California. Doug can be reached at dfisher@mail.sdsu.edu.

 **Nancy Frey, PhD**, is professor of educational leadership at San Diego State University and a teacher-leader at Health Sciences High & Middle College. A credentialed special educator, reading specialist, and administrator in California, Nancy is also the recipient of both the 2008 Early Career Achievement Award from the Literacy Research Association and a Christa McAuliffe award for Excellence in Teacher Education from the American Association of State Colleges and Universities. Nancy can be reached at nfrey@mail.sdsu.edu.

Nancy and Doug collaborate often. *Text Complexity* (IRA, 2012) and *Rigorous Reading* (Corwin Literacy, 2013), among their many best-selling texts, focus on how students can achieve a deeper understanding of complex texts with the right kind of instruction.

ABOUT THE CONTRIBUTORS

Heather Anderson is an English and higher-level Spanish teacher at Health Sciences High & Middle College. Heather earned her MA in Curriculum and Instruction from San Diego State University, is BCLAD-certified, has extensive experience in staff development, and spent part of her career as an elementary math specialist. Heather has shared her passion for education while presenting at conferences and consulting at individual school sites emphasizing the use of Gradual Release of Responsibility, differentiated instruction, close reading, and collaborative grouping.

Marisol Thayre is an English teacher at Health Sciences High & Middle College. She is interested in how students use different types of media to develop their own expertise as writers, and she has recently begun to share her knowledge with other teachers across the country as a presenter on topics that include close reading and the Gradual Release of Responsibility. Marisol earned her MA in English and Composition from Cal Poly San Luis Obispo and is BCLAD- and Leading Edge–certified.

A SAGE Company

Corwin is committed to improving education for all learners by publishing books and other professional development resources for those serving the field of PreK–12 education. By providing practical, hands-on materials, Corwin continues to carry out the promise of its motto: **"Helping Educators Do Their Work Better."**